KENT CHARACTERS

Wacky, Weird and Wonderful

Chris McCooey

By the same author:
Despatches from the Home Front
Sussex Heroes – Brave, Resourceful & True
Images of Southborough and High Brooms
Voices of Southborough and High Brooms
Kent Scandals – Sensational, Salacious & Sad
Rogues, Rascals & Rebels of Kent & Sussex

First published in 2002
© Chris McCooey
The moral right of the author has been asserted

Published by JAK Books
tel: 01892 529228
email: chris.mccooey@tiscali.co.uk

Front Cover illustrations - upright: Betty Bolaine,
top to bottom: Dr Dorrit Waterfield, Dr Hewlett Johnson and
Major Percy Powell-Cotton with unidentified pygmies.

ISBN 0-9524491-5-9

Reprographics this edition, SRS Graphics
01892 512440, art@srsgraphics.u-net.com

Printed by The Ink Pot,
South Bank House, Victoria Road, Tunbridge Wells, Kent TN4 0LT
tel: 01892 547799   email: info@theinkpot.com

CONTENTS

FOREWORD

Characters are, by definition, people who stand out a bit from the crowd — because of the lives they lived, their work, their exploits, even their physical appearance. This book records three dozen such people, all of whom have an association with the county, who are a bit different from the average man of Kent or Kentish man (or woman). Some of the characters are national or international figures, while others are hardly known within the county. All, however, have a story to tell and, hopefully, provide a stimulating and enjoyable read.

Chris McCooey

ILLUSTRATIONS

ACKNOWLEDGEMENTS

Much of the 'leg work' for this book was done by Bowen Pearse, a friend and fellow writer, who handed over to me all of his research notes on these characters. He saved me a great deal of sleuthing through archives and libraries and I am greatly indebted to him.

Others who have helped me, include, in no particular order, the following. The Dean of Canterbury, the Very Reverend Robert Willis, who welcomed me to The Deanery with tea in the shade of the great cathedral and allowed me to take photos of the bust of his famous, some would say infamous, predecessor – Dr Hewlett Johnson. Also thanks to Cressida Annesley, the cathedral archivist, and Margaret Sparks, a local Canterbury historian, who checked the chapter on the 'Red Dean'. Staying in Canterbury, I would like to thank Dr Frank Panton for helping me so extensively with the research on the city's great tycoon James Simmons.

Thanks too, to Dr Peter Waterfield, the nephew of Dr Dorrit Waterfield who checked the chapter on his remarkable aunt and sent me a photo of her. Also I would like to personally thank the Eldridge sisters, Mary and Ruth, the indefatigable pair who protect and cherish the legacy and collections of Denys Eyre Bower. Thanks, too, to Ron and Rene Vernon, the resident custodians who kindly showed me around Chiddingstone Castle.

The chapter on HE Bates was read by his son Richard, who generously supplied me with a photo of his father. John Harrison, the curator of the Powell-Cotton Museum at Birchington, kindly checked my chapter on the man who founded the collections at Quex House, and loaned me the photo of the major with the pygmies. As for the Salomons family who lived in Broomhill in Southborough, James Baldock, the marketing manager there, generously supplied me with pictures of the three Davids.

A big thank you to all the librarians, heritage officers and archivists who work for the Kent County Council who helped Bowen and I get hold of previously published material on these characters.

And finally thanks to Liz Howe for making the book look good with her computer wizardry.

I have done my best to give credit and acknowledgement to all who have helped me produce this book with research and illustration. If I have missed anybody out … apologies.

Chris McCooey, Southborough, Kent, November 2002.

Accidents Led to Literary Success

RICHARD HARRIS BARHAM (1788 - 1845)

In his day, the Reverend Richard Barham, who wrote under the pseudonym of Thomas Ingoldsby, Esquire, was as popular as Charles Dickens but today few people know about the Kent writer who was a master of comic verse. Yet because he was so popular in the 19th and early 20th century, his books selling in the hundreds of thousands, the chances of being able to get copies of the three books that made his reputation - *The Ingoldsby Legends* - are high indeed, if you frequent second-hand book and charity shops.

Richard Harris Barham was born at 61 Burgate in Canterbury on December 6th 1788 (the house was bombed during the Second World War but the building that replaced it has a plaque which reads: 'an unrivalled humorist, a poet, a genealogist, an antiquary, a clergyman greatly beloved'). The family name of Barham has a long association with Kent; indeed they gave their name to the village of Barham near Canterbury. The family claimed descent from a notorious knight, FitzUrse, one of the four who murdered Thomas à Becket in the cathedral in 1170. Following this dastardly deed, FitzUrse fled to Ireland and changed his name, adopting the Anglicised version - De Bearham. The family's fortunes fluctuated over the succeeding centuries but by the time the young Richard was born, in 1788, it was comparatively wealthy. His father, also

Richard Harris Barham

called Richard Harris, was an alderman of the city and a successful hop grower who had an estate, Tappington Hall, at Denton on the Folkestone Road.

Alderman Barham was Falstaffian in size - most sources say he weighed 19 stone, while one has him as 27 stone! Needless to say he liked to eat and drink; a favourite tipple was port and each evening it was his custom to drink a bottle of it.

The alderman had married his housekeeper, Elizabeth Fox, who was from Minster-in-Thanet and she seems to have imparted her sunny-nature and sense of fun to her son, Richard. But father and son did not have many years together as Richard senior died when his son was only seven - the alderman was of such girth that the door at No 61 had to be partly dismantled to allow the coffin to go in and come out.

Curiously Richard did not attend the local, King's School, but was sent to St Paul's in London. When he was 14, he was travelling on the Dover mail coach when it turned over and his right arm was badly crushed. For a time it was feared that he might lose it, but he recovered sufficient use of it to be able to write but not enough to play games. This may have dispirited many a lively teenager but Richard turned more and more to reading and writing because of the disability. He was a popular lad at school and for two years running he was elected the school captain.

From St Paul's he went to Brasenose College, Oxford to read law. Like many a student then, and since, he got heavily into debt - in his case playing, and losing, heavily at cards. Merry and mischief making came easily to the comparatively well off student and he hugely enjoyed his years at Oxford. When the time came to leave and get a job, he went to his guardian, Lord Rokeby, to lend him money from the family trust to pay off his gambling and other debts. The noble lord refused him a loan, but gave him the money instead, a salutary lesson which made the young man ponder on the true values of life. Instead of practising law, as he had planned, he changed his mind and entered the church.

This decision brought him back to his native county. His first curacy was at Ashford; he was 25 years old and the year was 1813. He married Caroline Smart in 1814 and while they were living at Westwell she bore him two sons; one died at seven weeks and there is a memorial plaque to him in the north wall of the sanctuary of the 13th century church. The other son born to them here, Richard Harris Dalton Barham went on to become a vicar too and it was he who wrote his father's biography. In all the Barhams had nine children and their father was to outlive six of them.

In 1817, Barham became the vicar at Snargate on Romney Marsh, but he was also offered the curacy of Warehorne and he and his family lived there. Two years later another accident forced him to concentrate his mind. He was travelling in a gig which overturned; he fractured one leg and sprained the other and while he was laid up in bed recovering from this serious accident he passed the time writing, by all accounts, an eminently forgettable novel titled *Baldwin*.

During his curacy of various parishes in Kent, Barham must have known that many of his congregation were earning more from illegal activities at night than from their honest toil by day. The infamous traffic of smuggling was rife during the first half of the 19th century - high taxes on supposedly luxury items as tea, tobacco and spirits meant that going to France and buying them at the market rate over there still left scope for a good mark up back in England. Although the authorities were beginning to tackle the problem by employing soldiers and sailors no longer needed to fight Napoleon, the Custom officers and the Blockade men had their work cut out. The sociable vicar would hear many stories of derrying do, and ghosts and spirits (of one sort or another) as mysterious gangs of men moved barrels and boxes of goods from boat to shore to hiding places at night. For a writer this was all grist to his mill.

Through his Oxford contacts, Barham was elected a minor canon of St Paul's Cathedral and the family moved to London in 1821. He found he had considerable leisure time on his hands, and he used it by writing, often late into the night, with quill pen and paper, by the light of a candle; he was very fond of cats and often had one sitting on his table or even on his shoulder as he wrote. He contributed about one third of the total articles to Gorton's Biographical Dictionary and regularly wrote for Blackwood's Magazine, with a tale of college life - *My Cousin Nicholas* - becoming particularly popular. His need for some external prompting in his writing career can be seen in the Nicholas book - he'd written a few chapters of this and they duly appeared in serial form in Blackwood's. When the readers of the magazine expressed their liking for the tale he had to write more chapters to finish the novel off.

His church career was also progressing. In 1824, he was appointed a priest in ordinary to the Chapels Royal, and soon afterwards was presented to the united parishes of St Mary Magdalene and St Gregory by St Paul's. With the aid of the Chapter, he restored and rearranged the valuable library of St Paul's in 1837. Three years later in course of rotation he succeeded to the presidency of Sion College, also in London.

And that might have been that, if he hadn't been loyal to an old school friend, a publisher called Richard Bentley, who had brought out his *Miscellany,* under the editorship of Charles Dickens in 1837. Barham had already made a name for himself among the literati of London for his wit and gaiety (he was a founder member of the Garrick Club). He had a felicitous ability to throw off humorous verse like: *She drank Prussic Acid without any water, and died like a Duke and a Duchess's daughter!* For Bentley's publication he drew on his knowledge as an amateur antiquarian and genealogist, and the folklore of his beloved Kent, as well as a rich and vivid imagination, to write stories which came to be known as *The Ingoldsby Legends.*

Barham's great skill was to mix fact and fiction so skilfully that the reader did not know the difference. He would quote from old Latin documents that had such *gravitas,* that were so intermixed with real and imaginary names, marriages and descents of persons that readers would write and request further information of what were thought to be genuine records.

The first legend to be published was *The Spectre of Tappington,* which of course owed much to Barham's time living on his father's estate. Another ghostly tale revolves round a poor cobbler and his encounter with the supernatural in the Norman keep at Canterbury, which combines much authentic history with Barham's fiction. One couplet gives an idea of his clever rhyming verse and describes the dilapidated keep: *'Resembling (to compare great things with smaller), A well-scooped, mouldy Stilton cheese - but taller'.*

In the *King's Scholar's Story,* little is based on fact. It tells about Nell Cook, a maid to a bachelor canon of the cathedral whose 'merry eye' had captured her wayward affections. One day a 'niece' turns up to visit the canon. Nelly, in a fit of jealousy, successfully poisons the pair of them with 'some nasty doctor's stuff'. The scholar goes on:

'The Canon's head lies on the bed - his "niece" lies on the floor!

They are as dead as any nail that is in any door!'

For her crime Nell was buried alive in the Dark Entry in the cathedral and here tradition says, her ghost roams, after sunset, on Friday nights.

The *Legends* display Barham's extraordinary command of rhyme and rhythm. The very first one he wrote for Richard Bentley - *The Nurse's Story* - is typical of the way he can swiftly set the scene in a few lines.

'On the lone bleak moor, At the midnight hour,

Beneath the Gallows Tree,

Hand in Hand The Murderers stand
By one, by two, by three!
And the Moon that night With a grey, cold light
Each baleful object tips;
One half of her form Is seen through the storm,
The other half's hid in Eclipse!
And the cold Wind howls, And the Thunder growls,
And the Lightening is broad and bright;
And altogether It's very bad weather,
And an unpleasant sort of a night!'

The Jackdaw of Rheims is one of a very few that does not have a Kent theme but it shows Barham's excellent sense of humour - and this is written by a man who was used to going into a pulpit to give a sermon.

'If any one lied, - or if any one swore, -
Or slumber'd in pray'r-time and happen'd to snore,
That good Jackdaw Would give a great 'Caw!'
As much as to say, 'Don't do so any more!'

The Smuggler's Leap is vintage Barham. It is based on a story that the author heard on the Isle of Thanet. There is a chalk pit there which is known as the 'The Smuggler's Leap' and it is said that a riding officer working for the Custom and Excise, one Anthony Gill from Sandwich, was chasing a smuggler on horse back but a fog came down and both went over the cliff and were found dead the next morning ... but there was only the smuggler's horse lying dead. In the version that appears in *The Legends,* Barham implies that Gill is so keen to apprehend the smuggler that he makes a pact with the Devil to give him a horse that will ride down his quarry.

'*Devil take me,*' again quoth Exciseman Gill,
'If I had but that horse, I'd have Smuggler Bill!'

The smuggler tries to get rid of Gill by shooting his horse but out of the musket ball hole comes not blood, but flame! - clearly supernatural. The story ends with a moral.

Never say 'Devil take me!'
Or, 'shake me!' - or, 'bake me!'
Or such-like expressions. - Remember Old Nick
To take folks at their word is remarkably quick.
Another sound maxim I'd wish you to keep,
Is, 'Mind what you're after, and - Look ere you Leap!'

In 1844, Queen Victoria paid a state visit to London and Barham, while watching the procession from a friend's window, caught a chill which developed into bronchitis. He kept on working but was clearly unwell. He tried various spa visits - to Clifton and Bath - but these were to no avail. He died in London on June 17th 1845, and was buried in the church of St Mary Magdalen, but later his remains were removed to Kensal Green.

He Fell in Love with Kent

H E BATES (1905-1974)

'**K**ent is like a mistress: infinitely lovely and variable, surly and delicious, warm and treacherous, infuriating and unforgettable.' Herbert Ernest, but known to family and friends always as H E, wrote these words which sum up his feelings for his adopted county.

The writer was born in the leather-working town of Rushden in Northamptonshire on May 16th 1905. Both his maternal grandfather and father, Albert Ernest, were shoemakers and his mother, Lucy Elizabeth Lucas, also worked in the leather industry. Herbert was the eldest of two boys and a girl and, as he was to write later, he 'grew up in an atmosphere of intense respectability ... My parents were never a farthing in debt; great was the pride they took, as my grandparents did, in paying their way ... My father pursued his passion for nature and the countryside, and incidentally fostered my own.'

From a local school H E won a 'free place' to Kettering Grammar School; he did not enjoy his time there and left at 16 having achieved a third class Joint Oxford and Cambridge University Certificate. For somebody who was to become one of Britain's finest 20th century writers, it was an underwhelming academic record.

Instilled with his family work ethic his first job earned him ten shillings a week as a junior assistant reporter with *The Northampton Chronicle*. Curiously for someone who had known from an early age that he wanted to be a writer, he came to dislike the job intensely and left to work as a solicitor's clerk. But he was writing in all his spare time - short stories, plays and novels.

His first, *The Two Sisters,* was published in 1926 by Jonathan Cape, having been rejected by nine others. Cape, who had only been in the publishing business five years, had wisely recruited as his chief reader and literary adviser Edward Garnett, one of the most perceptive critics and distinguished readers of his era who had already fostered the careers of Conrad, Galsworthy and D H Lawrence. Because of the androgynous initials, and presumably the subject of the novel, Garnett had reported to Cape that he had 'found another genius - a Miss Bates.'

H E may have been miffed to have been addressed as a Miss, but he was very grateful for the modest advance from Cape who already was getting a reputation for his parsimony. Garnett lived in Kent, on the edge of the North Downs overlooking the Weald and Bates often visited him there. Both got enormous pleasure from walking in the beech woods especially at bluebell time or along the leafy lanes in apple and cherry blossom time. Garnett, like Cape, had something of a reputation for frugality - it was generally believed that he watered down his sherry. Garnett's tutelage of the budding writer continued until his death in 1937; Bates later, in 1950, paid a touching and memorable tribute to his mentor with *Edward Garnett: A Personal Portrait.*

H E Bates

In 1931, H E published his fourth novel and in the same year married Marjorie Helen Cox, known as Madge. Her family were in Kent although she had been born in Northamptonshire and the newly weds began looking for a place to live near them. Both fell in love with an old granary in Little Chart - it was virtually derelict but it was to be the writer's home for the rest of his life. With his loving wife providing the creature comforts and a family of two sons and two daughters, The Granary was to become 'the still centre of the turning earth', as T S Eliot had phrased it.

Bates applied himself to his craft and would write until spots danced in front of his eyes and his hands trembled. His reputation as a novelist was far in excess of his sales and like many writers at the beginning of their careers, money was a problem and he would do other writing work to pay the bills - articles, short stories, book reviews. When he needed a break, or inspiration, he would garden or go for a walk in the countryside of the Weald or the North Downs or on the windswept Romney Marsh.

But his literary reputation was growing. His friend, Robert Lusty wrote about this period in the author's life. 'H E had already made memorable the character of Uncle Silas and was acclaimed as a brilliant new delineator of the English countryside and its people with both his novels and short stories. Yet it required both concentration and courage to pursue undaunted his craft of writing with a young family to educate and maintain ... It was the unshakeable foundation provided by Madge, 'The Granary', and the interests of his growing children which maintained the deep integrity and humanity of the man and his writing.' But curiously his novels at this time were still based in the Midlands, although Kent was providing him with the space and a base for his creativity.

This all changed with the outbreak of war in 1939. Dramatically Kent was in the front line and Bates before long was in an RAF uniform. It was to be a major development to his writing career as he had been called up, in effect, to write for Britain. Officially he was a flight lieutenant to Public Relations, Air Ministry; in reality his job was propaganda. He was to write short stories to keep the nation's morale up.

Bates was granted unusual freedom of movement and access to pilots and mechanics and other service men and women in the airbases that were spread all over the Southeast. By 1942, he had been promoted to the rank of squadron leader and, under the pseudonym of Flying Officer X, *The Greatest People in the World* was published, followed by *How Sleep the Brave*. The books immortalised 'The Few' who fought the Battle of Britain, mostly in the skies above Kent. Both were to become an enormous publishing success, which pleased his publisher, still Jonathan Cape, no end. For the first time books by H E Bates (albeit under his pseudonym) were going to bring to the publisher more than the original advance to the author.

But Cape missed out. His next full length novel - *Fair Stood the Wind for France* - which came out in 1944 was published by Michael Joseph who was to remain his publishers for the rest of his life. After Garnett had died, the relationship with his original publisher seems to have cooled.

Bates had had a good war and he found himself as a writer both popular and comparatively well off, and a long succession of best sellers followed which were chosen by book clubs, reissued by Penguin, translated all over the world. Many of his novels and short stories were made into films and his income was substantial, although this meant that there was little time for fallow periods as the demands of the tax man appeared insatiable.

Bates was somewhat ambivalent about the success - the financial freedom it brought allowed him to travel and to live well, but essentially he was man of reserve, happiest at home in the quietude of the Kent countryside, away from the *literati* scene in London and the social occasions that his writing accolades demanded. If he had not been a writer, H E would like to have been a painter; in fact, his wealth allowed him to form a valuable collection of French Impressionists. His descriptions of the Kent countryside could almost be paintings in words. Two of his lesser-known books - *The Country Heart* (1949) and *The Country of White Clover* (1952) - are paeans to the county he loved. He is naturalist, artist and poet under one cover as he writes about the blossom on the apple trees, the flight of a kingfisher, or the attractions of a Wealden village. 'The greatest part of the beauty of this piece of earth,' he writes, 'lies in the ceaseless variation it offers. As if Providence had not given Kent enough in the way of agricultural riches it gave the hop as a final measure.' Somehow his paean does not become a pain because of his honesty - for example, in trying to describe the temperament of a typical East Kent man, he crystallises it in one of Kent's own words - 'orkardness.'

H E's Kent credentials, already very strong, were cemented for all time in 1958 when the irrepressible Larkins family burst upon the scene in *The Darling Buds of May*. Bates is supposed to have got the idea for the characters when he was driving through a village in Kent and saw a family outside a shop eating ice cream and potato crisps. Pop and his common-law wife Ma were warm and funny and wonderfully Rabelasianly human. They had six children: Mariette (a combination of Marie and Antoinette), Primrose (born in the spring), twins Zinnia and Petunia (Ma's favourite flowers), Victoria (born in the plum season) and Montgomery (named after the wartime general).

Some contemporary critics were appalled that Pop and Ma were not married and had so many children; but the author and his publisher were not put off by this as the reading public loved the cast of characters and the story lines. Four more books of Larkins family adventures followed bringing Bates enormous financial and popular success.

The Larkins also attracted the attentions of Hollywood with 'The Mating Game' coming to the big screen in 1959 with Debbie Reynolds and Tony Randall as the main stars. A London stage version followed with Peter Jones and the BBC made a radio series. But it was not until the Larkins made the small screen that whole new generations of fans discovered the Kent family.

One of H E's sons, Richard, had sold the TV rights to a US company but when production was slow to start the rights were rescinded and bought by Yorkshire TV. With the close co-operation of Richard, a six part series came out in 1991. It was 'perfick' timing - the country was in a recession and in need of some light relief. The beautiful sunny Kent countryside of the 1950s and the slower pace of life and rhythm of the seasons was captured exquisitely on film. In the lead was David Jason who played the jovial Pop, Pam Ferris the roly-poly and fun-loving Ma and the unknown Catherine Zeta-Jones played their eldest daughter Mariette.

In the first episode, consternation is caused by the arrival of a naive Inland Revenue inspector who wants to investigate how Pop makes a living on just 22 acres. Befuddled by Pop's accounting logic, Charlie stays for lunch, falls in love with Mariette and becomes part of the family. *The Darling Buds of May,* thanks to the strong acting and gentle story line with no swearing or explicit sex, no car chases or violence, went straight to the top of the viewing figure charts with more than 20 million and stayed there for all six episodes, putting the likes of *Coronation Street* and *East Enders* in their place.

Two more series followed and Pop's favourite adjective -'perfick' - became part of the national vocabulary. In the episode where Ma takes to her bed and surprises herself, and Pop, by giving birth, the actual great grand daughter of H E, Daisy May Bates, was the baby the TV crew used in the filming.

In all H E Bates wrote more than 60 books - either collections of short stories, novels or non-fiction titles about the countryside. He also wrote plays and was a screenwriter. He adapted a novel by Sussex writer Sheila Kaye-Smith, *Joanna Godden,* (about a woman who runs a sheep farm on Romney March in Edwardian times which was filmed by the Ealing studio in 1947 with Googie Withers and Chips Rafferty in the lead roles with the title *The Loves of Joanna Godden*).

There were also three volumes of autobiography, the last appeared in 1972. A year later H E was awarded the CBE. The prolific and gifted writer who simply loved his adopted county of Kent died in Canterbury hospital on January 29th 1974. His remains are in the Charing Crematorium near Ashford.

Inventor of the British Seaside

BENJAMIN BEALE

Yᴼᴼ have to imagine the British seaside before it was the seaside - at least the seaside as we know it. No sun-bathers, few swimmers. Certainly no swimming costumes. Often, the sea front was no more than a place for beaching fishing boats.

Then, in the early years of the 18th century came Dr Richard Russell, who expounded the beneficial effects of sea-bathing. Many took his advice to heart and health-seekers flocked to watering places along the south coast. Brighton was first in about 1730, followed later by Ramsgate, Margate and Whitstable.

The idea of bathing was all very well but few were prepared to expose themselves to prying eyes. In about 1750, the first visitors began coming to Margate - to bathe and to drink sea water! Soon the fashion became a craze. Margate's few inns became fully booked most of the time and accommodation had to be sought in fishermen's cottages. But even this was insufficient - the locals soon realised there was money to be made from people 'taking the waters' and built new houses for them.

Advert for Beale's Bathing Machine

The sexes were well segregated. The men went into the water first. They were carried out some way in boats, then plunged into the sea from there. The ladies could then bathe nearer the shore. But few found this a really satisfactory arrangement.

A solution was provided by a devout Margate Quaker with an inventive mind called Benjamin Beale. His answer was the bathing machine, a kind of mobile changing room on wheels, with outside facilities for concealed swimming.

On the side facing out to sea was a tent like structure which shielded the bathers from peeping Toms. It was made of canvas or wood. The whole thing was drawn by a horse, driven by a so called guide. The earliest reference to Beale's bathing machine was in 1753, when it is described in a small handbook by an unnamed author. The booklet is called *A Description of the Isle of Thanet* and the frontispiece shows the general arrangement of the bathing machine.

The Poor Rate books of the parish indicate that in May 1754, Benjamin was assessed for a 'Mrs Baker's stables and hay loft' and it is thought he may have used these to store his bathing machines. But his business was growing and he had a tenement and workshop on the site of No 20 The Parade. Later he had to take additional workshop space.

In *All About Margate,* published in 1867, there is this detailed description of the bathing scene: 'The sea-bathing at Margate has the reputation of being far more animated than in any other part of the coast. There are a number of waiting rooms in the High Street where the customers retire until the machines are ready and which are fitted with every luxury, including yesterday's newspaper and a piano with a rich banjo tone'.

The author goes on to describe the bathing machine as having 'a very wet carpet inside'. He writes: 'When the box begins to move, we are sent bumping from side to side like a weaver's shuttle. At last we are in the sea with the waves splashing up against the machine and making a gurgling noise among the wheels and shaking the door as if they are trying to come inside and wet our clothes.'

Beale is generally considered to have been the inventor of the bathing machine in this country but it is thought the idea was borrowed from France. In the previous century, on August 2nd 1651, a man by the name of Evelyn wrote in his diary: 'I went with my wife to Conflans, where were an abundance of ladies and others bathing in the river; the ladies had their tents spread on the water for privacy'. This of course was exactly what Beale provided in his machine.

Soon other seaside towns adopted Beale's machines and, according to an 1831 guide-book, they were also exported to such places as to the East and West Indies.

Charges made to the public were: lady taking a machine, guide included 1/3; two or more ladies, guide included, 1/- each; two or more young children, guide included, 9d each; gentlemen taking a machine, guide included, 1/6; two or more gentlemen, 1/3 each; two or more gentlemen bathing themselves, 9d each.

There has been some speculation (but apparently no written reports) as to what the bathers actually wore, if anything. It seems likely that the men simply stripped off and swam naked. But the ladies - both before and after the invention of the bathing machine - probably put on the same clothes as they wore in Bath when taking the waters there. These were 'garments made of yellow canvas which is stiff and made large with sleeves like a parson's gown'.

It was just as well the ladies swam in this or any other get-up. For, according to one report, the town was full of voyeurs. 'No one was without his spy-glass until the whole coast bristled with these nautical contrivances, which were quite as often seen pointing towards the machines as towards the fishing vessels'.

A lot of words have been written about Benjamin Beale and his bathing machines but little detail about Beale's life. A few simple facts are known. He was born in 1717, the son of a glover and breeches maker. On December 5th 1731, at the age of about 14, he was apprenticed to Abraham Bubbers, a 'wheeler' of Greenwich. Despite this, Benjamin seems to have gone into his father's business for in his will, he is similarly described as a 'glover and breeches maker'.

In 1740 he married Elizabeth Bindlock of Canterbury. The couple had no children or if they had, none survived.

Despite the success and popularity of his bathing machine, Beale, like many inventors, before and after him, gained little material reward. A succession of storms damaged or destroyed most of his machines and bathing rooms and brought near ruin to their owner. A public subscription was organised by two prominent citizens, Sir John Shaw and Dr Hawley. This may have helped Beale to buy Draper's Farm in 1771, but he was virtually broke when he died in May 1775, at the age of only 58.

His widow, Elizabeth, spent the rest of her life supported by charity in the Draper's almshouses. She lived to the grand old age of 92 and was buried at Draper's Hospital, Margate on April 28th 1806.

The bathing machine business was carried on by members of the

Beale family well into the 19th century. According to *The Picture of Margate* by W C Oulton, published in 1820, there were six bathing houses near Garner's Library in the High Street, and one was the property of Messrs T Hughes and J Beale.

In an article from the *Isle of Thanet Gazette* for October 21st, 1936, the author, Sir Ambrose Heal, reports on research carried out on Benjamin Beale's early family history. According to this account, the Beale family originally came from Antwerp in the early part of the 14th century and set up as weavers in Kent.

The first Beale of note was of Maidstone. He had 21 children and died in 1399. He is honoured with a commemorative plaque on the wall of the south choir aisle of All Saints, put there around 1599. According to the vicar of All Saints, Christopher Morgan-Jones, over the years there were a number of prominent Beale men, including several mayors.

Towards the end of the 19th century, somebody copied a piece of graffiti, thought to have been written by a grateful woman bather, on the inside of one of Beale's machines. It seems a fitting tribute.

Though oft have I been
In a bathing machine,
I never discover'd till now,
The wonderful art
Of this little go-cart
'Tis vastly convenient, I vow
A peg for your clothes,
A glass for your nose,
And, shutting the little trap-door,
You are safe from the ken
Of those impudent men
Who wander about on the shore.

'I Live Still to Love Still Things Quiet and Unconcerned'

EDMUND BLUNDEN (1896-1974)

Although born in London at 54 Tottenham Court Rd, Edmund Charles was brought up in Kent. The future poet's parents were both schoolteachers and they had moved to Yalding in 1900 and Edmund's four brothers and three sisters were all born in the Kent village during the next decade. Edmund's father, Charles, served for 12 years as church organist and is remembered by a brass plate on the side of the organ console. He was also a fine left arm bowler and served as secretary and treasurer for the village cricket club for many years.

With two teachers as parents it is not surprising that Edmund showed aptitude at school. Before the move to Yalding the family lived at Framfield in Sussex and the school register shows that he attended the infants' school there (his mother was the headmistress), when he was only three. When the family moved to Kent he went to a dame school run by two ladies in Yalding and then transferred to the village's Boys' School where his father was headmaster. His mother was the headmistress of Yalding's Infants' School and is said to have taken six weeks' leave before the birth of each of her children and six weeks' leave afterwards. The family lived in the school house for eight years - this is now part of the Lower School; externally the building has changed little since the Blundens' time.

In 1907, Edmund transferred to Cleaves Grammar School, which used to be on the north side of the village green in Yalding. Two years later he won a scholarship to Christ's Hospital School, near Horsham in Sussex and became a Bluecoat. He did well academically, becoming Senior Grecian and was also popular enough to be elected head boy. In 1914, he won the senior classics scholarship to Queen's College, Oxford but did not take it up - instead he went to war, volunteering for the 11th Battalion, Royal Sussex Regiment.

Blunden's experiences of life in the trenches profoundly affected him both as a man and as a writer. He was to become a pacifist because of the horrors that he saw at first hand, although his personal bravery accounted for him being commissioned in 1916 and being awarded the Military Cross in 1917. He wrote an account of his service in Flanders later and

Edmund Blunden on being awarded the Order of the Rising Sun

Undertones of War, a prose account of life in the trenches, was to become a classic. He felt an intense loyalty not only to his immediate comrades in the Regiment but to all of his generation, without respect to nationality, who had shared the hell of life at the front, and was haunted throughout his life by its memories. It was in France that he first had an asthma attack, a disease that stayed with him all his life and eventually killed him.

Not surprisingly, after being demobbed, he found it hard to settle back into academic work. He had gone straight from school to become a soldier after all. He tried to take up his scholarship at Oxford in 1919, but left a year later without a degree for London to become assistant to Middleton Murray on *The Athenaeum,* which merged with *The Nation* two years later under the editorship of H W Massingham. As well as contributing to this publication Blunden had two collections of poetry published - *The Waggoner* in 1920 and *The Shepherd* in 1922. It was these two collections that made his name as a poet, with the latter collection being awarded the prestigious Hawthornden Prize .

In 1923 a chance meeting was to lead to Blunden being inextricably linked to Japan for the rest of his life. Takeshi Saito, a distinguished scholar of the English Literature faculty at the Imperial University in Tokyo, had met Blunden at the London home of another poet, Ralph Hodgson, and he persuaded him to go to the Far East to teach. Blunden was somewhat reluctant but it seems to have been his destiny right from an early age.

Blunden recalled a meeting that he had had with an old shopkeeper in Yalding and wrote about it in the poem *Looking East.*

'Down our street when I was a boy I met with
a friendly man
Who took me to the stone-cross steps and said
To me, "See Japan."'

The young lad did his best to see, straining his eyes to the East, but he could not make out the old man's 'Mountain' in the clouds (Mount Fuji) and told him so.

'He smiled, and said I should find all out, and
the words that he left me were these:
"I come from my shop to see Japan, and the Mountain,
when I please."'

Leaving his wife Mary and their two surviving children (Joy, their first born daughter had died of a fever when only a few months old) back in England, Blunden arrived in Japan in April 1924. The pink cherry blossoms must have been the few splashes of colour in a landscape that must have been depressingly familiar to an ex-soldier. Two-thirds of the capital had been destroyed in an earthquake and catastrophic fire just seven months before.

Despite the dislocation caused by reconstruction, Blunden began teaching immediately. He amused his students by wearing a dark-brown homespun coat and a battered grey broad-rimmed hat, bent down at the front, not only to class but sometimes in class as well, as the temporary rooms used for teaching invariably had broken windows and inadequate heating at best. Sometimes he lectured in the Medical School where he shared the platform with a real skeleton.

One day Blunden and his students were with King Lear in his distress when a frightening rumbling roar and strong tremor forced everyone to dive for cover under their desks. Shattered glass from skylights rained down and when the dust began to settle and the noise had died away, the professor emerged from under his desk with a puzzled smile; but he was not unduly disturbed, as might be expected from a veteran of the trenches.

If his manner amused his students, then his scholarship and generosity in sharing it certainly impressed them too. One contemporary said his lectures were so popular that he was "like some Victorian revivalist preacher, filling a huge hall to bursting with a rapt congregation." As a teacher, he helped and encouraged with an open heart and a generous nature. This also seems to have been the case in his private life too.

According to Sumie Okada, the author of *Edmund Blunden in Japan,*

Blunden met a 36-year-old junior high school teacher of English, Aki Hayashi. She was well past the conventional marrying age in Japan and the poet was in a foreign country a long way from home and hearth. They began an affair and Miss Hayashi was led to believe that she would be the next Mrs Blunden.

After teaching for three years in Tokyo, Blunden returned to England. The professor committed the folly - reminiscent of Shelley, whom he so much admired, in its impetuousness and unintentional cruelty - of bringing Miss Hayashi with him as his 'secretary'. Once she was here, a secretary (without the inverted commas) is what she soon became, beavering away for him, year after barren year, in the British Museum Reading Room. By all accounts he became more and more perfunctory in his attentions and more and more dilatory in the payment of her meagre wages. When she predeceased him, Miss Hayashi left the carefully hoarded sum of £2,000 - all that she possessed after years of living in drab bedsitters - to her adored employer in her will.

Blunden's marriage to Mary was falling apart and for a time he moved back to Yalding to stay with his parents whose retirement home was Cleaves House, part of the former grammar school. In 1931 he divorced his wife and the same year became a Fellow of Merton College, Oxford and taught English literature. He married Sylvia Norman, a novelist and critic in 1933 but this ended in divorce in 1942 and he married for the third, and last time, Claire Poynting in 1945. During the next decade they had four daughters.

Blunden was back in Japan in 1947 as part of the UK Liaison Mission and during the next 28 months he gave over 600 lectures from Hokkaido in the north to Kyushu in the south on English literature and culture. This effort was a major contribution to the revival of English studies in the country. His great sympathy for a war weary people also added to his reputation - he was unflagging in giving of his time and his talents, never refusing requests to speak or to write a poem.

On one of his trips from Tokyo, Blunden travelled down the Izu peninsula to Ito to dedicate a poem to a fellow countryman who had been born in Gillingham, Kent. Will Adams, whose real life was the inspiration for James Clavell's classic adventure story *Shogun*, was shipwrecked in Japan in 1600. He eventually gained the confidence of, and became adviser to the supreme military dictator of the country Ieyasu Tokugawa and was made a samurai. Blunden unveiled a monument in 1948 to the man from Kent.

'Here then, while Shakespeare was with us, came

An Englishman to win a different fame ...
Come where Will Adams led the pioneers
Of ship design in Ito ...
I know his home in England and I know
At last his home by the Pacific's flow
And am most happy, thinking of that man
Who first united England and Japan,
Happy to find that spirit flowering still
Which set your garland on the brow of Kentish Will.'

Cricket was one of Blunden's passions and he was a walking Wisden when it came to players past and present. In 1944, his *Cricket Country,* a book about the game he loved, brought cheer to many during the troubled war years. In it he discourses on the great exponents of the game: W G Grace, C B Fry, Hutton and Hobbs and including Kent players such as Blythe, Hardinge, Ames and A P F Chapman. He also recalled colourful accounts of Kent village cricket including his own exploits and those of his cricketing friend and fellow poet Siegfried Sassoon of Brenchley.

While in Japan after the war he used to set up stumps in the garden of his house in the compound of the British Embassy adjacent to the Imperial Palace. Other expatriates went there to turn their arms over and keep their eyes in, like Australian journalist Richard Hughes who was correspondent for *The Times* and distinguished Japanophile Lewis Bush who retired to East Grinstead in Sussex. The warmth and wit of the likes of these three together and their banter concerning maidens and short legs, byes and silly mid-ons, must certainly have bewildered the Japanese who dropped in to talk of stanzas and sonnets, poetry and prose.

In recognition of his bridge-building between Britain and Japan Blunden was elected an honorary member of the Japan Academy in 1950 (he was made a Commander of the Order of the British Empire CBE in 1951) and in 1963 Emperor Hirohito inducted him into the Order of the Rising Sun, Third Class.

In the early 1950s Blunden was back in Kent living in Tonbridge and commuting to London to work for *The Times Literary Supplement* and in 1953 he went back to the Far East as professor of English Literature at the University of Hong Kong, where he taught for the next decade. During that time he visited his beloved Japan another six times to lecture and to ensure that he got supplies of Japanese bottled beer sent to him in Hong Kong.

In 1964 he returned to England and retired to Hall Mill, Long

Melford in Suffolk where he died on January 20th 1974. Edmunds parents are both buried in Yalding churchyard and in 1964, apparently without ceremony, a road in what is still called the 'New Estate' was named Blunden Lane. In 1979 an engraved window was placed in the south chancel wall of Yalding church in memory of the pacifist poet. Designed by Lawrence Whistler, it combines the horror of war with the peace of the Kent countryside, the barbed wire spikes becoming a living briar and the shell bursts becoming tress in bloom. Children from the village school were present at the dedication and one of the school's four houses is called Blunden.

'Of Parsimony, Vice, Avarice and Depravity'

BETTY BOLAINE (1723-1805)

The full quote is taken from the frontispiece of a pamphlet written just after Betty had died by a 'friend' of hers, one Elizabeth Burgess, who in life had tried to get her to change her ways.

It reads: *Life & History of Betty Bolaine, (late of Canterbury), A Well Known Character for Parsimony and Vice, scarcely equalled in the annals of Avarice and Depravity interspersed with Original Poetry.*

"*An immoderate desire after riches is a poison lodged in the soul; it contaminates and destroys every thing that was good in it; no sooner taketh root, than all virtue, all honesty, all natural affection, fly before the face of it. Where covetousness reigneth, know that the soul is poor*" (*Economy of Human Life*).

The poetry of La Burgess is execrable but the story that she tells of Betty Bolaine is fascinating, written both as an expose and as a warning with a high moral tone.

Elizabeth was born into a wealthy and much respected Canterbury family. Her father was Noah Bolaine, an apothecary, who was happy to spend money on giving her a fine education. Being young, attractive, talented, and from a good family, it's not surprising that when the time came for her to enter society she had many admirers. The fact that her

Betty Bolaine

father had died and left her £1,500 (a small fortune in the middle of the 18th century) also added to her attractiveness.

But along with a naturally pleasing manner, her chronicler records that she possessed considerable artifice, constantly requiring her suitors to pay for her entertainments and hinting broadly that a particular present would be gratefully received. She would also borrow unashamedly from her friends: money, clothes, jewellery - and not return them. Betty quickly got the reputation as a tease, leading men on and then dumping them.

Once at the Lord Mayor's Ball in London (wearing a dress borrowed from the lady with whom she was staying), Betty danced so elegantly that she captivated a captain in the Royal Navy who immediately proposed marriage. Captain E (in the 18th century, the convention was to just use the first letter of the surname when relationships were written about) seems to have thought that she had agreed; Betty, on the other hand, had other ideas. According to *The History:* 'But the wary nymph, averse to any engagement that might shackle her fortune and liberty, kept him still at bay, dallying with his passion, but accepting his presents.'

The naval officer got so exasperated with the wilful woman that he determined to carry out the marriage ceremony by taking her aboard one of His Majesty's ships and getting the captain to conduct the ceremony, a practice considered legal back then. With his brother's help they enticed her into a carriage and headed for a ship riding at anchor on the Thames. Betty would have none of it, once she realised what was going on, and threw such a tantrum with loud hysterics that passers by in the Strand rescued her. As for Captain E: 'Not more mortified than astonished at her inconsistencies, made her his farewell bow and sheared off.'

Another gentleman of Canterbury, one Joseph G, became engaged to her but considering her track record, he wisely persuaded her to sign what might be considered a pre-nuptial agreement. If the marriage did not take place she was to pay him a bond amounting to £200. Betty was in a bind but she chose her moment carefully to extricate herself. Her fiancé had been invited to 'an assembly, given by a general then stationed in Canterbury'. Betty could have gone too, but decided not to as she had been ridiculed at a previous party in the city when she had turned up in what she thought was the height of fashion - a hoop petticoat. If it had been made by a dressmaker that may well have been fine but she had made it herself from a few strips of cane, tied with common string and covered by an old blue apron that had belonged to her late father.

Betty said to Mr G that if he really loved her he would spend that evening with her. This led to an argument with Betty ranting and raging and accusing her husband-to-be of having another lover. She pulled out a knife, conveniently blunt, and made to plunge it into her heart, knowing full well that the thick whalebone stays of her corset would prevent any real damage. Horrified, her fiancé wrestled the knife from her but in so doing Betty's hand was badly cut and a surgeon was immediately summoned to stitch her up.

This tempestuous incident seems to have cleared the air. In the kiss-and-make-up process she confirmed her intention to marry him and all preparations were made. On the appointed day at a church within walking distance of where Betty was living in Burgate, the minister was at the altar with family and friends in the pews. Just before setting off to exchange vows, Betty inveigles the bond from her husband-to-be. Mr G proceeds to the church, so that his bride can follow and make her triumphal entrance. But Betty had no intention of going through with the ceremony and destroyed the bond. At the church the jilted groom waits in vain. After an hour he realised he has been duped and, mortified, Mr G left the church, and Canterbury, never to return.

Betty's cruel and scheming ways were not confined to her dealings with men. Her family suffered too. Her poor mother went in fear of her daughter who supposedly looked after her in a long illness. Once Betty was out for the day and her mother craved a mutton chop. Despite her illness she went to the butcher and bought one and was cooking it on a gridiron when Betty unexpectedly returned. The daughter flew into a rage, slapped her own mother and threw the chop onto the floor and stamped on it.

In contrast to Betty, her brother, who also lived in Canterbury, was universally respected and loved. He had married a Miss Farnham, a sister to the Countess of Denbigh, by whom he had a most beautiful daughter. Her niece was timid and was bullied awfully by this harridan of an aunt, who duped her brother and sister-in-law into letting her spend time with her. According to Betty's biographer, her cruelty towards her niece 'was in a great degree, the occasion of her death in the bloom of life.' (Betty had even forged her mother's will to deny a legacy of £500 that she had left to her son).

Next to be in thrall of this mentally unstable woman, was a man some 40 years her senior - and rich. She set her sights on Mr H's bank balance and events were proceeding smoothly towards matrimony when 'the enamoured swain refused to settle the whole of his fortune on her'. Despite this setback she considered it was to her financial advantage to live with the man. Unfortunately Mr H had a family and Betty was so unpleasant to them that he agreed to rent a large house for his common-law wife to live, complete with servants, while his children stayed on in the family home.

Mr H often visited Betty in the rented house, but her parsimonious ways had not deserted her. One evening, the frail old man dared to complain that the meal that she set before him was very small and not at all appetising. She flew into a rage and pushed him down the stairs. The fall and his old age made him ill and he took to his bed. His family came to visit him and telling Betty that they were going to give him some fresh air took him away for good.

Betty was outraged and considered suing him for £2,000 in damages, but wisely gave up the idea. The old man died soon after and in his will left her £50 and a horse drawn vehicle. She thought this not enough and sent in an enormous demand, which the family completely ignored.

Next on the scene was a Mr M. Betty offered him accommodation (she was still living in the house rented for her by the old man) while his own property was being renovated. Mr M was somewhat miffed when he moved out to be presented with a huge bill, even though he had paid all the housekeeping expenses, during his stay. Nonetheless, he paid and Betty banked it straight away.

Surprisingly, considering her notoriety, paramours continued to appear. Next in line was Mr B and before too long Betty was living with him and also agreed to assume his surname. He was as mean as she was and quite content to supper on a mouldy crust and burn old cabbage stalks and other rubbish from the garden on the household fire instead of wood and coal.

Mr B was a gardener who had a house at St Lawrence in the Isle of Thanet, which they would rent out in the summer. If they went there by wagon, they would invariably save money by pulling hay from other peoples' stacks along the way and feeding it to the horses.

When it was necessary to go up to London to bank some money or check on other investments, Betty would walk or scrounge a lift on a wagon or coach. She was quite happy sleeping under a hedge. She loved a nip of gin and if she could not beg this from friends she spent good money to buy it, her only extravagance, it would seem. She was always dressed as if she was a poor woman with her rags patched with rags; this allowed her to stay at the Richard Watts Charity almshouse at Rochester where poor travellers could get a bed, two meals and four pence to send them on their way the next day. Another time she looked so destitute that the master of the Gravesend to London ferry allowed her to travel free. She used these London visits to deliver letters from people in Kent and built up a network of acquaintances in this way, skilfully trying to deliver them just as they were sitting down to a meal to which she hoped to get an invitation. If she was travelling up to London in winter, she would allow Mr B but one scuttle of coal, and instructed him to stay in bed to keep warm.

Mr B seems to have lived in fear of Betty, lamenting to friends that he had often tried to end his miserable existence. When he was on his deathbed, she fed him cowheel broth, perhaps the least nutritional soup imaginable. As soon as he had drawn his last breath she set off for his house in St Lawrence where she picked over the property of his that she wanted. Upon her return, she could not bear to see a shroud wasted on a corpse and removed it to make a petticoat. The naked corpse in a coffin was sent unattended to his relations at Ramsgate who paid for his funeral. Betty borrowed a mourning bonnet from one of his relatives to pay her respects; needless to say she never returned it.

The gardener had written a will. In it he had left his son a shilling, even though the son's godmother had willed a £1,000 to him 'provided his father approved his conduct'. Betty had persuaded Mr B that the son's conduct was unacceptable so securing the £1,000, in effect, for herself. The son begged Betty to let him have some of his property - all she would agree to was letting him have a portrait of his father. As for the money of the old gardener, the will stated that it should go to Betty's niece in trust, with Betty named as the sole trustee.

But there was a complication. Old Mr B had been a bankrupt and after he died, the creditors came looking for their money from the person who was known as his wife, Mrs Betty B, although of course, they had not gone through with an official wedding ceremony. She seems to have panicked as she went up to London and withdrew all her common-law husband's money out of the bank and also cashed in her own investments. She concealed £8,000 on her person and caught the Gravesend ferry back to Kent. The journey was not to her liking: 'The weather being boisterous, she was so far intimidated as never again to venture by water.' Nobody paid her any attention so the money was perfectly safe because she was dressed as a mumper, or beggar.

With the creditors closing in she thought of going to live in France but then came up with a cunning plan: she made all of her property over to her niece. The creditors could go and whistle! When they realised they had been out-smarted they gave up. Straightway, Betty went to her niece and demanded the money back, and it was refunded without hesitation.

Her remaining years were spent in squalor, living in 'a small and miserable habitation' which she refused to repair. Dishes caught rainwater in the bedroom; she used this for her drinking water, as she never required water for any other purpose. She struck up a friendship with an old cobbler who lived in Wincheap and would go and visit him most days - he would boil water for her breakfast tea and if she was there at supper time (as she invariably was) he'd stand her a meal as well. He often gave her books to read, of which she was very fond, particularly delighting in those relating to the history of misers. It seems that the old cobbler enjoyed her companionship as *The History* says: 'of nothing was she liberal but her company.'

Betty was a regular churchgoer but even there she was stingy. One day, having received communion at All Saint's Church, the clerk apologised for missing her when he went round with the collection plate. She said not to worry, as she would be seeing poor people as she went back home, implying that she would give to them!

She never washed herself nor her cooking pots. If she had been visiting someone at night she always begged a candle for the walk home and as soon as she was in the street she would blow it out. She was not averse to pilfering from her friends: pins, threads, tape, paper, pens. She was also a shoplifter - she was caught stealing a pound of bacon from the butcher's stall in the market, but managed to jest her way out of that tricky situation. People who had the temerity to come to her for charity were got rid of by her grabbing a broom and sweeping the house - it was so filthy that the dust raised forced people to quickly get fresh air.

Betty died in her sleep in her 83rd year. The inquest said she had died by the visitation of God. Apart from £100 to the Kent and Canterbury Hospital, three five guinea and a dozen one guinea legacies to family and friends, the whole of her estate, amounting to £20,000 she bequeathed to an honorary canon of Canterbury Cathedral, the Rev Dr Walesby whom she'd only known for a few weeks. He is reputed to have spent this fortune indulging himself in 'a princely manner'. To the poor woman who had attended Betty for many years, there was nothing.

Betty had requested that the bell be tolled for an hour and that a hatchment be placed over her house to record her life. When this dwelling became an apple store, the joke was often repeated; 'Good fruits from Betty's house never came before.' The funeral itself was chaotic - Betty was so unloved that people showed no respect, no one wore black and the coffin was jeered at as it was taken away to be interred in a vault within St

Mary Magdalene in Burgate Street. The church was pulled down in 1872 but a tablet to her memory is incorporated into the base of the tower that remains.

Elizabeth Burgess wrote a damning epitaph:

'To pity, deaf! Tho' large her store of gold,
When misr'y knocked, she never op'd the door;
Of her, it never can with truth be told,
She cloathed the naked, or she fed the poor.'

Buddhist Who Fell for a Fake Countess

DENYS EYRE BOWER (1905-1977)

Denys Eyre Bower was born in 1905 into a well-off Derbyshire family; his father and grandfather both held high positions in the London Midland and Scottish railway. Although he did not inherit money from his family (certainly not enough to buy a castle), he certainly inherited a love of fine art - Denys's father was a collector of Chinese porcelain. Denys joined the Midland bank after leaving grammar school when he was 17 years old and his modest, but steady clerk's income allowed him, over the next 20 years to build up the basis of his collections. During the economically difficult years of the 1920s and 1930s an astute collector could pick up quality items for a song. If he couldn't get time off work, Denys would send a 'runner' to the auctions to bid for him. He appreciated any object that was well crafted but specialized in four areas: Stuart and Jacobite memorabilia (including part of the heart of James II), Japanese lacquer ware and samurai armour, Ancient Egyptian artifacts and figures of Buddha (Bower himself was Buddhist).

In 1942 he moved to London, and set up as an antique dealer at No 2 Baker Street. He began to make a name for himself as a knowledgeable buyer at auctions and all dealers considered him absolutely trustworthy. In 1956, he bought Chiddingstone Castle in Kent for £6,000 with a 100% bank loan. Owned and lived in by the Streatfeild family from the early 1500s to 1948, the building had metamorphosed from an old manor house into a fine red brick Caroline mansion and then into a romantic castle, surfaced with sandstone blocks and with towers and turrets, crenellating and embattling, sometime around 1800. It was this 'castle' that Bower bought and he opened it with his collections to the public, hoping to earn a living and pay off the debt to the bank. The building was in such bad repair that he could hardly, quite literally on occasions, keep his head above water; the roof leaked so badly in wet weather. Later on he commented wryly: "the trouble with white elephants is that they come cheap but have voracious appetites."

His salvation came, or so he thought, when he met Anna Grimaldi, daughter of one of the Grimaldis of Monaco who said she was the widow of the Comte d'Estainville and had fled to Peckham in London to escape the attentions of her family who was pestering her to marry again. 'Naïve' and 'gullible' come to mind, as Bower's friends could clearly see that she was an imposter - she got away with not speaking French by saying she was in England to practice her English. Denys was star-crossed when it came to affairs of the heart - he had already been married twice before - an Italian Jew during the war and a Danish girl in the 1940s, but neither marriage had lasted long and both ended in divorce.

Anna and Denys became engaged in 1957 but the Comtess (in reality the daughter of a Peckham bus driver) broke it off when she realised that the castle owner was not as rich as she thought (one wonders, who was kidding whom?)- in fact he had no money, just a huge debt. Denys went up to Peckham to remonstrate with her, carrying a handgun which he had acquired by chance when he found it in the drawer of a desk that he had bought at auction.

He intended to deliver an ultimatum: if she did not marry him, he would blow his brains out in front of her. When she refused, he pulled the gun out to carry through with his threat but it went off accidentally. The Comtess collapsed in a pool of blood. He thought he had killed her. He turned the gun on himself, but instead of putting it to his head, he pointed it into his stomach and pulled the trigger.

Denys Eyre Bower

When he came to he was in hospital, having had his spleen removed in an emergency operation, and a policeman was next to his bed. He was charged with attempted murder and suicide (still a crime then). He was sent for trial, found guilty and given a life sentence. The tabloids had a field day with headings like: CASTLE OWNER SHOOTS FINANCÉE.

Denys, although protesting his innocence, accepted his sentence and spent the next five years in Wormwood Scrubs. He was taught bookbinding in prison and in spite of his disability - he'd fallen off his motorbike in his youth and a lorry had run over and crushed his right hand (which accounts for why he was not called up in the war) - he spent his time binding his collection of Stuart and Jacobite pamphlets, a collection considered to be the finest apart from that held by the British royal family.

Needless to say the bank was concerned about its loan to the man serving time at her Majesty's pleasure and this is where Ruth Eldridge and her sister Mary come into the story. Ruth had trained as a solicitor and she had followed the case in the newspapers and felt strongly that a miscarriage of justice had taken place. An article written in *The Sunday Pictorial* that she considered to be libelous also incensed her, suggesting that Denys came from a family with a long history of insanity, in effect that he was a nutcase.

"It was Destiny. I had to take the case on," Ruth recalls. "It seemed to me that kicking a man when he was down may well be the best time to kick him, but it was so unfair. My Scottish mother taught me to believe in Providence and that you accept that you have a duty to do some things and that is what I did."

With full power of attorney while Bower was incarcerated, Ruth set about the daunting task of keeping the collections together and trying to make the castle weatherproof. To say the place was a mess was an understatement. Cobwebs, dust and dirt, dog muck (two had run free in the house for years), damp walls, pilfering by visitors and caretakers - all had to be dealt with.

By physical hard work and judicious selling of items deemed not essential to the core of each collection, the castle limped along until the time came for Bower to be released under license. (Ruth was particularly pleased that a libel action against *The Sunday Pictorial* was won and that the paper paid damages of £9,750).

Denys came back to live in Chiddingstone and began to play his part, still going to auctions when something caught his eye as well as showing visitors around; he never let on to them that the collections were his pride and joy and that he owned the castle (or rather the bank did). Locals recall him as reserved if not aloof, and he lived in stately squalor, neither tidying nor cleaning his private quarters. He could not resist a bargain, even for groceries. Late on a Saturday he would drive his Rolls Royce into Tunbridge Wells and buy up reduced items; in fact he seemed to live on streaky bacon and over-ripe bananas.

Despite his prison ordeal, his humour remained intact - his neighbour Lord Astor of Hever Castle once invited him on a pheasant shoot but he politely declined by saying: "My shooting days are over."

Ruth was still involved too, keeping an eye on the finances of the place and supporting Denys. (She had tried to dissuade him from buying the Rolls but, for once, had failed to get her way; Denys had borrowed £650 from his bank manager to pay for the 1947 Silver Wraith). Her sister Mary explained the relationship: "It was obvious that Denys could not survive on his own. He took appalling risks financially, but to abandon him would be rather like letting go of a drowning man that you had just rescued, and leaving him to drown. Besides he was a genius in his way, working like a tornado, yet always very quietly and patiently in a blinkered way, obsessed with his collection. He always said he was not creative, not original. But he was truly an artist, and like many artists he needed an impresario."

Gradually visitor numbers began to increase until by the middle 1970s there were 30,000 a year. In 1977 Denys was taken ill with cardiac asthma and died after a short illness. Prior to his death Ruth had suggested he make out his will leaving the castle and his collections to the National Trust, not outright but as Trustees; he thought that the National Trust would be only too pleased to have the castle to go with the village of Chiddingstone, which it already owned. After some initial interest in the bequest the National Trust declined the gift, mainly because there was no lump sum endowment with which to run the property.

It seemed that the collections would have to be broken up and the castle sold off for flats, or some similar development. But again Ruth, ably assisted by her sister who acted as secretary in all the legal paper work, came to the rescue. A niece of Denys Bower claimed that Denys's sole wish was that the National Trust should have Chiddingstone Castle and believed, as this was not possible that there was an intestacy and as next of kin, that she should inherit all of her uncle's property. Ruth maintained that there was a general charitable intention, that if the National Trust did not want to be trustees then others might. The case went to the High Court and Mr Justice Oliver ruled in 1979 that the 'devise and bequest were valid charitable gifts so the castle should be run as an independent charity.'

And this is in fact what has happened. With Ruth a life trustee plus six others (including a representative of the National Library of Scotland to monitor the Stuart and Jacobite collection and one from the British

Museum to keep an eye on the Egyptian collection), Chiddingstone Castle continues to shine as a beacon of English eccentricity.

As Ron and Rene Vernon, one of three couples who act as custodians, said: "Many stout hearted men would have run away from this place - but these two ladies, Ruth and Mary, have carried it on their shoulders."

Watchmaker Turned Inventor

LOUIS BRENNAN (1852-1932)

Louis Brennan

Although Louis Brennan is not a household name, he played an important role in the development of three famous inventions in the late 19th and early 20th centuries: the torpedo, monorail transport and the helicopter. This versatility was part of his genius and he deserves to be remembered. Despite a successful career as a mechanical engineer and inventor, his personal life was desperately sad. Maybe his work provided an escape for him.

Brennan was born in Castlebar in County Mayo on January 28th 1852. When he was nine, he emigrated to Australia with his mother Bridget and father Thomas and the family settled in Melbourne. The young Louis was already showing an aptitude for problem solving, as most of his toys were either mechanical or scientific - he delighted in taking them to pieces and seeing how they worked.

Whilst still at school he was already inventing: a safety catch for a window, a billiard marker (an idea which he sold), an incubator and a compound steelyard weighing machine. He also made a large clock, a kind of mini-Big Ben, which was put in a public place for people to tell the time. Indeed it was while working as a watchmaker that he came up with his first big idea - a dirigible torpedo.

The idea had come to him by chance. He realised that it was possible to make a machine travel forward by pulling it backward and demonstrated this by using a cotton reel with a pencil thrust through the hole in the centre and resting the ends of the pencil on two books. When he unwound the cotton, by pulling it from underneath, the reel rolled away from him, and the faster the cotton unwound, the faster the reel moved. He thought of various applications for his idea but the only vehicle that he could think of which required driving for a limited distance and did not have to make the return journey was a torpedo. If then, he reasoned, you substitute for the reel a steel cylinder carrying an explosive charge, and replace the cotton with piano wire, you have the Brennan Dirigible (i.e. capable of being directed or guided) Torpedo.

The year was 1874, so Brennan was just 22. A Melbourne businessman, John R Temperley, persuaded him to form a company and with other backers on board as well, the Brennan Torpedo Company was formed. A patent was taken out in February 1878 and a working model was successfully tested the following year in front of an audience of politicians, journalists and naval and military personnel.

To make the most of the invention, Brennan had to get it accepted by a super power so he and Temperley travelled to London in 1880. Naval and artillery officers inspected the dirigible torpedo at Woolwich. They advised against its use from ships but recommended that trials be carried out from shore-based forts, where it could be used in harbour defence. The Commandant of the School of Military Engineering, Sir Andrew Clarke, was sufficiently impressed as well to recommend the construction of an improved pattern at Government expense.

Brennan and Temperley were paid £5,000 for their expenses to date and the inventor retained on a fixed salary of £1,000 for three years. In order to be near his place of work, Brennan moved into The Cottage, Gillingham Green. Here was close to the experimental station that had been established at Garrison Point Fort, Sheerness and the workshop at the Royal Engineers HQ at Brompton Barracks between Gillingham and Chatham.

After satisfactory trials, Brennan was in a position to invite the Government to purchase the copyright to his invention. This is where Temperley took over, as he was an expert negotiator. Brennan conceded later that he would have settled for much less than the sum actually secured. After hard bargaining, payment of £110,000 was agreed spread over three years. Some thought this an astonishing amount of money but others argued that the technology had to be kept away from foreign, possibly hostile, governments. Although he may not have been as good a negotiator as Temperley, Brennan was a pretty shrewd investor. He insisted that the Government pay him in gold bars and each year he went in a horse and dray to the Bank of England to collect payment.

The torpedo could be propelled and directed from the shore by two reels each capable of holding up to six miles of fine steel wire. Each weighed 3 $^1/_2$ tons, and had a range of 1 $^1/_2$ miles carrying an explosive charge of 200 lbs of wet guncotton. The reels were driven by high-pressure steam engines, at a speed of 30 mph with the torpedo at a depth of ten feet. One of Brennan's torpedoes can be seen in the Royal Engineers Museum at Brompton Barracks in Gillingham.

In 1887 Brennan was appointed superintendent of the government factory at Gillingham, which manufactured the torpedo. This factory was in operation until 1906 when this type of defence was superseded by shore batteries of 9.2 inch guns, speedier to operate and with greater range and directional manoeuvrability.

In 1892, Brennan was awarded the CB (Companion of the Bath) for his services to military defence and he also married Anna Mary Quinn of Castlebar. Once married he bought Woodlands House in Gillingham, which had 12 acres of grounds and was on an elevated site overlooking the Medway. In 1896, he stepped down from his position as superintendent at the Gillingham factory and became a part-time consultant instead. This allowed him time to work on his next invention - the gyroscope monorail based on the simple concept of the child's spinning top.

Brennan's inspiration for this went back to his time in Australia, a country with vast distances between towns and cities, which needed a rapid overland travel system across rough country which also had to be economic. Consequently a single rail would be the cheapest method if it were possible to balance a train on it. When on holiday in Cannes, he had purchased a simple gyroscope from a street pedlar giving demonstrations of its use, and he used this as a basis for his invention.

Early experiments were tried out in the workshops attached to his private home Woodlands House and in December 1903 he was sufficiently satisfied with progress that he took out a patent, No 27, 212. As finance became a development problem, Brennan reached an agreement with the War Office whereby he was granted funds, and the right to use the torpedo factory machinery and staff, in return for which the government department would be able to use the completed invention on favourable terms.

A complete working model of a railway vehicle with an overall length of six feet was set up and built to one eighth scale and the track on which it ran was laid out in the grounds of Woodlands House (this is now in the Science Museum in London). Brennan took great delight in transporting his daughter around the grounds once he had solved problems of overheating gyroscopes and lubrication of bearings. By 1909 he had built a full-size vehicle, which could seat 50 people on benches, and he began giving public demonstrations most notably at the Japanese-British Exhibition at the White City from May to September 1910.

In November of the same year Winston Churchill, the Home

Secretary, arranged for the Prime Minster, Lord Asquith, and other ministers including Lloyd George, the Chancellor of the Exchequer to view a trial demonstration of the gyro-monorail. Despite showing interest, the politicians felt it was a commercial decision and even though the national press gave an enthusiastic endorsement, the project was not taken forward, partly no doubt, because the various railway companies were committed to travel by dual rails and the cost of conversation would have been considerable. Brennan had sunk all of his private fortune into this project and so was very disappointed when it was abandoned in 1912, the same year that he left Gillingham.

Brennan worked on classified government business during the First World War, inventing and developing munitions. From 1919 he worked for the Air Ministry at the Royal Aircraft Establishment at Farnborough, developing a helicopter flying machine, an idea that had first come to him in 1884. Despite Churchill's interest in this project the Brennan driven rotor helicopter was abandoned in 1926, but not before it had proved itself to some degree. It had shown adequate lifting capacity and the fact that about 70 free flights of an average duration of two to three minutes had been carried out in the open, was surely evidence of a measure of control. His valediction to the abandoned project proved prophetic. He wrote: 'The helicopter will be found of great value, once it is in existence, for many purposes that are now unthought of, such as parcel and mail collections and deliveries in cities, passenger carrying and also, by the combined action of several machines, for lifting and carrying heavy weights over all impediments to elevated points if desired.'

As well as his government work, Brennan had also come up with practical inventions for use in everyday life. He told a work colleague how he invented the Brennograph. "I get quite a lot of ideas during the night and I have to switch on my light to make notes, which awakens my wife, so I feel I must have a means of making notes in the dark and it must be silent and require a minimum of movement to operate." Eventually he produced a small machine that could easily be carried and operated in a jacket pocket. It had just five keys, and letters and symbols were produced by combinations of these keys being pressed, rather than struck, so it was therefore silent.

Another invention was a power-operated means for ascending stairs. This again was born out of necessity as he suffered badly from asthma and so he had this fitted in his Gillingham home, Woodlands House.

With the demise of the helicopter project, the inventor appears to have slowed down. He was 73 years old. He had already lost one of his two daughters in the influenza outbreak of 1919. Added to this tragedy, his wife had mental health problems. His son, too, suffered - he was forced to give up a promising Army career and died at an early age in a mental institution. Brennan's remaining daughter also lived her life in a mental institution.

On Boxing Day 1931, Brennan was on holiday in Montreux in Switzerland when he was knocked down by a car and he died three weeks later. He is buried in the family grave at St Mary's Cemetery in Harrow Road, London.

A View in Kent He Loved Best in the World.

JOSEPH CONRAD (1857-1924)

For 20 years Joseph Conrad had lived a venturous life sailing throughout the world as a merchant seaman but when the time came to settle down and write it was Kent in which he chose to live and work. All of his great books - *Lord Jim, Typhoon, Nostromo* - were written in rural Kent. Although based on his strange and exotic experiences in the jungles of Africa or the spice islands of Southeast Asia, it was looking out over the Weald that provided him the peace and quiet that he needed to write. But perhaps the most extraordinary aspect of the man was that he was writing not in his native language (Polish), nor even in his second language (French) but in English, which he had taught himself.

Conrad was born on December 3rd 1857 in Berdichev, which then was part of Poland but is now in the Ukraine. He was christened Josef Teodor Konrad Nalecz Korzeniowski. His father, also called Josef, was from a wealthy landed Polish family and was a well-known man of letters, having translated Shakespeare into his native language. He was also a teacher of French and he taught his son a second language. Young Conrad's fascination with the sea may well have come from his father who had translated Victor Hugo's *Les Travailleurs de la Mer* - Joseph junior would read aloud to his father about the seafarers.

When he was only five years old, Conrad's comfortable life changed dramatically. His father had been implicated in the Polish rebellion of 1862 and he was banished to Siberia. Although not actually destitute, the family was exposed to continual discomfort and in great spiritual misery. The anxieties of this time hastened the death of Evelina, his mother, in 1865. Two years later the widower and his son were allowed to leave Russia and they settled in Lemberg in Austrian Galicia. Father and son became very close but the relationship did not last long; in 1869, Josef senior died and the 12-year-old boy was placed in the guardianship of his uncle, with whom he went to live in Cracow.

In 1874, speaking fluent French, Conrad went to Marseilles and signed on to become a registered seaman in the French merchant marine. He used the experiences and escapades during this time, as he did for all his time at sea, to provide him with characters and plots for his later writing.

Four years after first going to sea, he transferred to the British merchant marine and began to learn English. In 1886 at the age of 28 he assumed British nationality and changed his name to Joseph Conrad. In November of the same year he passed his 'ship's master' examination which meant he could captain his own ship.

In 1889, Conrad began writing a story, rather as an alleviation of boredom, than any ambition toward authorship. The manuscript travelled around with him under his pillow in his bunk for several years, slowly increasing in length. Twice it was lost, but fortunately found again. In January 1894, he decided to come ashore for the last time and try and make it as a writer. He spent several months putting the final touches to his manuscript and then sent it to the publisher T Fisher Unwin, who passed it to their reader and critic Edward Garnett, who immediately recognised it as the work of a major new writer. *Almayer's Folly* was published in 1895.

In March 1896 Conrad married Jessie, daughter of a bookseller, Alfred Henry George and their first home was in France, on the Brittany coast but in September the same year they were back in England. They rented a number of properties in the Southeast before moving in 1898 to Pent Farm, in Postling, a tiny village near Hythe. Another writer, Ford Madox Ford, had been the previous tenant and it was here that Conrad pronounced: "This is the view I love best in the world" - a view south across rolling farmland to Romney Marsh and the sea.

Conrad quickly became one of the *literati* of Kent and Sussex and the writers would visit one another. H G Wells lived at Sandgate and would cycle over to Postling; the first time he called caused quite a stir as he was such a literary giant

Joseph Conrad

and Conrad was just beginning to establish his reputation. Jessie had prepared a fine meal but when he did arrive, half an hour late, all Wells could manage was a glass of milk and two aspirin.

Rudyard Kipling was not far away in Burwash and Henry James lived in Rye. Edward Garnett had a house on the edge of the North Downs and was a frequent visitor; Ford Madox Ford became a friend and they collaborated on three books, two of which *The Inheritors* and *Romance* had a Kent setting. Most of Conrad's novels and short stories had rather exotic locations based on the time he spent at sea but one had a completely Kent setting and that was *Amy Foster* - it is about a Polish sailor who was shipwrecked on the Kent coast and the countryside is painted in somewhat sombre shades.

When John Galsworthy came to stay he would get off the train at Sandling Junction and walk briskly to Postling. Other guests would be met off the train by Conrad who would take a pony and trap to pick them up. He would encourage the Kent-born and bred animal in his native Polish much to the delight of his passengers. Later on he changed this means of transport for a Cadillac and then a Humber and would drive around the Kent lanes 'quite recklessly' according to one contemporary account.

The farmhouse at Postling provided seclusion for Conrad to get on with his writing. When he needed a break he would walk the short distance to Stanford and would chat with the landlord of the Drum Inn, an ex-mariner, about their seafaring days. Conrad's wife was not so keen about the primitive plumbing and the house's isolation but she stoically looked after the writer and was pleased to welcome guests who provided company for her. While they lived at Postling the Conrads had two sons.

In 1907 the lease on Pent Farm ran out and the Conrads moved away from Kent for 18 months. Jessie described the move as a "temporary aberration of mind" and all the family appeared relieved to move back to The Cottage at Aldington for a short spell (the squeals from the nearby abattoir were a bit disconcerting) and then to Capel House, a moated farmhouse at Orleston, near Ashford in 1910. Conrad described this place as his "sylvan wilderness". Two other moves followed - for a short time in 1919 they lived in Spring Grove in Wye and the writer's last home was Oswalds (now The Rectory) at Bishopsbourne.

Although he was acclaimed by his fellow writers, Conrad's novels and short stories did not bring him much popular success. Money, or rather the lack of it, was a constant worry and his health suffered. He came close to a complete nervous breakdown but despite depression he doggedly persevered in his craft, cutting himself off in his study from family and friends for days at a time and chain-smoking furiously. In his own world he acted out the lives of his characters with a passionate intensity. Jessie recalls one day standing outside the house talking to the gardener, when the window of his study was thrown open and Conrad thrust his head out. His voice was hoarse, and his appearance dishevelled. The gardener was scared witless. "She's dead, Jess!" "Who?" I asked, suddenly feeling sick. "Why, Lena, of course, and I have got title, it is *Victory!*"

Financial success came in 1914, when his novel *Chance* was picked up by the American publisher F N Doubleday and for the next ten years, until his death in 1924, Conrad was more discussed, praised and written about in England and America than any other living writer. He died of a heart attack on August 3rd and his funeral was held in St Thomas's Roman Catholic Church in Canterbury during Cricket Week and he is buried in the city's cemetery

Although somewhat out of fashion today, he is the undisputed prose-laureate of the sea. His worship and defiance of the mistress-tyrant will mean that Joseph Conrad's name will endure.

Painter and Parricide

RICHARD DADD (1817-1886)

One August morning in 1843, two butchers from Rochester were going by horse and cart through woods in Cobham Park to Wrotham to buy livestock at the market there. They noticed someone laying face down in the grass as if sleeping off the effects of a heavy night. They decided to see if he was all right; Charles Lester left his uncle Abraham Lester tending the horse and went over to the sleeping body. When he could not be roused Charles realised he was not dead drunk, but plain dead.

A shepherd, George Biggs, had been in the woods looking for some lost sheep and came over to see what was going on. The two men turned the body over - the victim had had his throat cut and he'd also been stabbed several times in the chest. There was a lot of blood on the body and around it.

Abraham decided to go and get the village constable in Cobham. Soon William Daws, the part-time officer of the law, had shut up his tailor shop and was at the scene of what was clearly a murder. He searched the crime scene with John Adams, a waiter from the Ship Inn who straightaway recognised the victim as the man who had come to Cobham the evening before. He had known Robert Dadd for 12 years; the family had lived in Chatham for several generations and Robert had had a chemist's shop in the High Street. Dadd was with a younger man whom he said was his son Richard.

Richard Dadd

The night before Adams had waited on them at table and then went and found lodgings for them to spend the night in Cobham. The two men said they would go out for a walk and Adams waited up for them to show them where they were going to sleep. When neither had returned by midnight, he went to bed. The constable was already getting a pretty good picture of the events leading up to the murder.

At the crime scene, they found the victim's hat and walking stick, as well as a large razor and a knife, both blood stained. In the pockets of the deceased, was £2 17s 6d and a gold fob watch - robbery, clearly was not a motive. They noticed that the grass had been trampled down as if there had been quite a fight.

After a while, the body was taken to Cobham and placed in the wheelwright's shop, near the Ship public house and William Saunders, a surgeon from Gravesend was summoned to perform a post mortem. He found bruises on the wrist and two punctures to the lungs made by a knife through the ribs. It was the surgeon's opinion that because of the nature of the wounds the victim had not committed suicide.

At the inquest, the coroner heard that the son Richard had disappeared. He recognised that from what they knew, they had not the slightest evidence to connect the son with the murder, although there appeared to be a great deal of suspicion. The coroner considered the best and safest course for the jury to pursue would be to return a verdict of wilful murder by some person or persons unknown, which they duly did.

If the coroner's jury did not know who committed the murder, other members of the Dadd family were in no doubt. They were seriously concerned about the mental health of Richard and were worried when their father had said he was going on a trip to Cobham with his son. After the murder, the family and friends of the Dadds' arranged to have printed, published and circulated a handbill offering a £10 reward. It caught the attention with MURDER! printed in bold letters and then went on: 'Missing a young man about 24 years of age, labouring under insanity, and named Richard Dadd.' Although it did not accuse Richard of the murder, in fact it mentioned that he may have met with the same fate as his unfortunate parent, most people who knew the man were in little doubt he was the killer.

The press was in no doubt too. Soon every newspaper in the country was thrilling readers with the horrors of the crime under the headline: DREADFUL MURDER AND PARRICIDE AT COBHAM PARK. There was a great deal of speculation about where the murderer might be. Some thought that he must have taken his own life by throwing himself in the Thames. One journal spoke about the 'late Richard Dadd ... for although the grave has not actually closed over him, he must be classed among the dead.' Other rumours suggested he had hired an open boat in Dover or even spoken to friends in Oxford Street. The fact was he could not be found.

Richard Dadd was not exactly an unknown person; he had already begun to make a name for himself as an artist. He had been born in Chatham on August 1st 1817, the fourth child of seven. His father Robert, the murder victim, practised as a chemist and his father's father had been the timber master to the dockyard responsible, among other duties, for refitting *Victory* before the battle of Trafalgar. Robert was keenly interested in adult education, a good lecturer, and in politics known as 'a staunch reformer'. His first wife, Richard's mother, died when the boy was six and his father married for the second time and she bore him two more sons. But in 1830 the family was once again left motherless upon the death of his stepmother; from then Mary Ann, Robert's eldest daughter took care of the family, cooking and doing the chores. There is some speculation that this traumatic upbringing may have unbalanced the children; four of the nine were to die insane.

By all accounts, Richard was his father's favourite and had a pleasant disposition. He attended the King's School in Rochester and began to show interest in, and talent for drawing in his early teens. In 1836 his father sold his chemist's business and the family moved to London, where he took over a water gilding and ormolu business and very quickly had achieved the status: By Appointment to Her Majesty The Queen.

The London home was in Suffolk Street, Pall Mall, conveniently near the Royal Academy, which was just then in the process of moving from Somerset House to the recently built National Gallery. Richard entered the Academy Schools in January 1837 at the same time as William Powell Frith, later to be seen as the epitome of High Victorianism, and John 'Spanish' Phillip. Henry O'Neil and Augustus Egg were already students, and together these five formed the nucleus of a loosely knit group calling itself 'The Clique'.

Richard, in retrospect, was seen as one of the most diligent and promising students at the Schools. He won a number of silver medals for his painting. He exhibited landscapes in 1837 and two years later one of his paintings *Don Quixote,* was bought by the well-known Irish actor and comedian Tyron Power who was the great grandfather of the American action adventure film star of the same name. Another commission was to decorate panels in Lord Foley's house in Grosvenor Square. One scene from *Manfred,* a dramatic poem by Lord Byron, depicted tortured spirits and demoniac hauntings - the poet described his work "as a sort of mad drama ... a Bedlam tragedy", which was to prove prophetic for the painter.

In 1842, Richard's career was given a tremendous boost when Sir Thomas Phillips engaged the young painter to accompany him on a Grand Tour of Europe and the Middle East. His job was to record scenes and make an illustrative record of their journey. Richard set off with Sir Thomas on 16 July. The painter was on the threshold of a great career, he was charming and intelligent, handsome and gifted and the trip augured nothing but pleasure and success. Ten months later he returned home alone and quite clearly ... mad.

The journey started in Ostend and then they travelled through Belgium, Germany, Switzerland and Italy. The usual troubles occurred - fleas in beds, over-zealous customs officials at borders - but they pressed on through Greece and Turkey to Asia Minor and by the end of November they were in Cairo. By this time they had had enough of rough living in tents and travelling by horseback and Sir Thomas hired a boat with a crew of 16 from the English consul at Cairo and proceeded up the Nile going ashore to inspect all the antiquities. They would breakfast on fresh eggs and boiled ham and on Christmas Day dined on plum pudding. Richard became increasingly absorbed in Egyptian religion and mythology while Sir Thomas would amuse himself by shooting crocodiles.

In Egypt, Richard appeared to suffer the attack of sunstroke, which was afterwards blamed for all his troubles. It was slight and he recovered. Although his subsequent behaviour did give some cause for concern, it was not enough to hasten the homeward journey and a full month was spent in Rome. But Richard was fighting off the terrors of approaching madness - he believed an external power was telling him to attack people who were the devil incarnate. When he saw the Pope, this impulse gripped him but he did not attack him as the Papal Guard was so strong.

In Paris, Richard's self-control broke completely for the first time and Sir Thomas decided he needed medical help. Before this could be arranged Richard left the city on his own and fled to London where he threw himself into his painting. His friends were seriously worried - he was prone to outburst of violence and self-mutilation, and his behaviour became erratic so much so that his landlady went in fear of her life. He lived exclusively on eggs and ale.

The one person who was quite unable to accept that anything was wrong beyond the aftermath of sunstroke, which rest and quiet would cure, was Robert Dadd, the painter's father. But the son was already plotting his father's murder. He applied for a passport and bought a razor with a knife with a spring blade. Psychiatrists today would no doubt diagnose paranoid schizophrenia but back in the middle of the 19th century the best that could be done was for a doctor to agree that the patient was no longer responsible for his or her actions and must be constantly supervised.

But hospitalisation in a secure place was not to be - at least not for the time being. Richard persuaded his father to accompany him to a favourite sketching ground of his childhood, Cobham Park. Later Richard used the word 'inveigle' in describing how he had got his father to join him - which reinforces the idea that the murder was premeditated. Having left the pub for a walk, Richard attacked his father and tried to cut his throat but actually killed him by stabbing him in the chest.

The murder took place soon after 9pm as an hour later Richard was at the Crown Inn at Rochester where he went to an upstairs room to wash the blood from his hands. A chambermaid, Eliza Coleman, remembered that the colour of the water afterwards was very dark, but could not tell whether with blood or mud. The fugitive then engaged the inn's postilion, Charles Overy, to take him in a two-horse chaise to the George at Sittingbourne. Overy remembered Dadd because he had asked him to drive faster and was quite mean with the tip; he paid him 2s 6d over but the driver considered 5s would have been fairer as it was so late at night. Dadd got another postilion to take him to Dover where he immediately took a boat to France as he had his passport with him.

Dadd headed south by coach and when going through the forest of Valence, he tried to slit the throat of a fellow passenger. Overcome with remorse, Dadd tried to defuse the situation by offering him money, but he was arrested and confessed to a local magistrate that he had killed a man in England under direct orders from the Egyptian god Osiris. He was committed to Chermont Asylum, where he remained until he was extradited back to England.

Twice Dadd appeared before magistrates at Rochester where he certainly looked mad according to the *Rochester, Chatham & Strood Gazette*. His hair was long and his beard full and bushy and his wild eyes darted about, and he often interrupted the proceedings, challenging facts and accusing others of the murder. Richard Dadd was ordered to be transferred to the State Criminal Lunatic Asylum then at Bethlem Hospital in St George's Fields, Southwark (his brother was a patient in the Incurable Establishment of the main hospital but they never had any contact).

Dadd spent the rest of his life behind bars, but he continued to paint, producing some of his best work, thanks to the enlightenment of the doctors who treated his illness and their belief that it was good for their patient. His paintings from this period include *Dymphna Martyr* (St Dymphna is the patron saint of lunatics), *Oberon and Titania* and *The Fairy Feller's Master-stroke* (now in the Tate) - both considered to be masterpieces of depiction of the world of fairies. The landscapes that he painted were drawn from memory, of course, but often these would include scenes from Kent with the Medway and Rochester Castle often in the background.

In 1864 all the criminal patients were transferred to the newly built Broadmoor Hospital. There Dadd continued to paint with astonishing versatility: murals, stage sets, furniture decoration, painting on glass and even diagrams and illustrations for lectures. It is amazing that paintings of such technical perfection and beauty could be created out of the squalor and ugliness of a 19th century criminal lunatic asylum.

Richard Dadd died of tuberculosis in 1886 and was buried in the grounds of Broadmoor. There is no headstone or mark left of his grave as the cemetery area has now been made into a lawn.

Evolution by Natural Selection

CHARLES ROBERT DARWIN (1809-1882)

Charles Darwin - who lived 40 years of his life in the Kentish village of Downe - changed the way we think of ourselves and where we come from. Before the publication of his *Origin of Species* and *Descent of Man,* the Christian world had the cosy belief that God created man and all other beings and that all these species remain unchanged forever. After Darwin, most people were convinced that the Bible was merely myth - that we were all in fact descended, aeons ago, from a common ancestor.

In earlier times, Darwin would have probably suffered a rather unpleasant death for damning the Bible wrong. It is perhaps a sign of the times - the late 19th century - that the world was ready for Darwin's message. At his death, he was universally mourned.

Charles was born on February 12th 1809, at The Mount, Shrewsbury, the son of Robert Waring Darwin and grandson of Erasmus Darwin. His mother had been Susannah Wedgwood of the famous pottery family. Apparently little was expected of the young Charles. The lad was mortified when one day his father said to him: "You care for nothing but shooting, dogs, and rat-catching and you will be a disgrace to yourself and your family".

Charles' mother died in 1817 when Charles was eight years old so that, to some extent, his education was left in the hands of his elder sisters. It was a happy childhood and always in later life, he held fond memories of his home and father.

In 1817 he went to a day school, under a Mr Case, minister of the unitarian chapel where, as a boy, he had attended service. In the summer of 1818, he became a boarder at Shrewsbury School under Dr Butler. He learned little outside of the classics but worked diligently at chemistry in an amateur laboratory his brother had set up in the tool-house at home - a study that his school disapproved of. Even at this stage of his life, Charles was an ardent collector of almost everything - franks, seals, coins, minerals, animals, plants and other natural history objects. He was encouraged in this by a book, *A Natural History of Selborne,* and it was a habit that in the future, was to make him an ardent coleopterist.

He later recalled that as a child, he had pulled off the bark of a tree and discovered two rare types of beetle. Discovering a third, he put one beetle in his mouth. However, in protest, the beetle squirted such a foul-tasting liquid, that Charles had to spit it out.

The first choice of career was to take after his father in medicine and for this he joined his brother at Edinburgh University. But Charles showed little interest in the subject and - in the days before chloroform - was horrified by the operating theatre.

Much to the disappointment of his father, Charles gave up all idea of being a doctor and arranged to study for the next-best career, that of being a priest. In 1828, he went up to Cambridge to obtain the obligatory Bachelor of Arts. Later he recalled: "I did not then in the least doubt the strict and literal truth of every word of the Bible".

Charles Darwin

Despite his preference for shooting partridges rather than attending lectures, he did pass his final examinations, coming tenth in the poll. However, he was compelled to return to Cambridge to make up the proper time of residence before he could get his BA. He had already struck up a friendship with Henslow, professor of Botany. They used often to walk together and Charles gained the sobriquet of 'the man who walks with Henslow'.

Another great influence at this time was the book, Humboldt's *Personal Narrative*. It raised in him a passion for natural history and the travels of naturalists. Henslow now persuaded him to study geology. This led to a geological tour of North Wales. On his arrival home, he found a letter from Henslow, recommending him to take the position of an unpaid botanist on the *Beagle*. Henslow stressed that Charles was just the man for the job. Charles would have jumped at the offer but was at first held back by the refusal of his father. Dr Darwin was prevailed upon to let his son go and finally permission was granted.

On December 27th 1831, Charles Darwin set sail on the 235-ton sloop-brig *HMS Beagle*. This fantastic voyage was to take five years and make Darwin a new man. But Charles was unable to take part in the initial festivities - as he was seriously seasick.

He gradually recovered from his sea sickness and in the rain forests of Brazil, he was enraptured with the abundance of wild life. It also gave him much cause for thought. He unearthed the bones of the extinct giant sloth and found they were similar in shape (although much larger) to the small sloth alive today. Where had these giant beasts been at the time of Noah's great flood?

Even more mysterious were the bones of a horse. When the Spanish conquistadors arrived in the 16th century, the horse was unknown in South America. Yet here was definite proof that they did exist in the remote past. Did this mean that various species were constantly changing and those unable to adjust to their environment died out? If this was the case, the species alive today must be very different from those that God originally created. There was even doubt that creation could have lasted only seven days; creation was a continuous process that had been going on for a considerable time.

On the Galapagos Islands, Darwin saw creatures found nowhere else on earth. And it was here that Darwin's momentous ideas - a challenge to everything believed before - began to form. The general scientific belief had always been that species never changed. But here on the Galapagos, he found great changes. For example, there were varying forms of mocking-birds, tortoises, and finches on different islands.

He realised that the ideas now buzzing around in his head challenged Christian man's most basic beliefs. All the accepted theories about the origins of life would have to be revised. It would mean that the Book of Genesis - including the stories of Adam and Eve and the Flood - was no more than a collection of myths.

The *Beagle* journeyed onto Tahiti, where Darwin loved the plants and animals and was intrigued by the simple lifestyle of the people. This was in marked contrast with what he found in New Zealand and Australia. Here the local people had been subjugated by the European settlers. This supported his theory of the animal world - that the stronger always took over from the weaker.

It is impossible to exaggerate the importance of the *Beagle* trip to Darwin. He had left England untried and almost uneducated. He returned a successful collector, a practised and brilliant geologist with a wide knowledge of zoology in many parts of the world. But above all, his theories on evolution had begun to grow in his brain. The first step had been taken on the road to the *Origin of Species*.

The *Beagle* returned to Falmouth on October 2nd 1836. Darwin spent the next few years organising and cataloguing his vast collections of plants, animals, rocks and fossils, many of which had been sent back to England, from various places during the voyage.

In 1838, he married his cousin Emma Wedgewood of the famous pottery firm. In the following year, he published his first best-seller, *Journal of Researches into the Natural History and Geology of the Countries Visited during the Voyage Round the World of HMS Beagle*. He had become a member of the Royal Society and was respected as a scientist and author. In the same year, he made his move to Kent, to Downe House, near Bromley.

It took Darwin some two decades before he published his *Origin of Species*. Poor health slowed him down but , most importantly, he wanted to be absolutely certain he had sufficient back-up material. During the 1840s and 1850s, he continued to work at Downe House. As his health worsened, he took to working for shorter and shorter periods. He walked in the gardens of his house and took carriage rides. His illness was never identified though it was thought he may have caught something like Chagas's disease (a kind of sleeping sickness spread by insects) on his round-the-world voyage.

He was becoming more and more convinced that species were not fixed and immutable. They changed. He talked to pigeon fanciers who bred new kinds of pigeons. Darwin called this 'artificial selection'. In 1855 he began to keep pigeons of his own, carrying out cross breeding. He wrote to various experts, having long discussions by post. Friends pressed him to bring his book to a conclusion.

Yet still he hesitated at publication.

In June 1858, Darwin received a letter from Malaya that was to change the world. It was from another naturalist called Alfred Wallace. With the letter was Wallace's own summary of his own theory of evolution, *On the Tendency of Varieties to Depart Indefinitely from the Original Type*.

Darwin was amazed to see that Wallace's work paralleled his own. Even Wallace's terms stood out as headings for Darwin's chapters. The two scientists read out their work at the Linnean Society in July 1858. Wallace advised Darwin that, as he (Darwin) had produced considerably more material, then he should produce the book. Wallace agreed to stand aside. *The Origin of Species* was published on November 24th 1859.

Darwin noted: 'Oh, good heavens! the relief to my head and body to banish the whole subject from my mind!'

John Murray, the publisher, had had only 1,250 copies printed and these were sold out in a day. The second edition (3,000 copies) was published on January 7th 1860. Letters poured in to Downe House. Many prominent figures agreed with his theories. But there was also a barrage of opposition, both at home and abroad. One clergyman called the mild mannered Darwin 'the most dangerous man in England'.

The Descent of Man followed in 1871. In this Darwin concluded that man, like the rest of the animal kingdom, had evolved and that all could be traced back to common ancestry in prehistory. In the public reaction, Darwin expected a hurricane and got a breeze. Between the years 1859 and 1871, their had been a change in public attitude. It seemed the world was now more ready to consider Darwin's theories.

In some countries, like Imperial Russia, the book was banned. At home, *The Times* thundered against the book and there were some who agreed with the Welshman who called him 'an old ape with a hairy face'. But as Adrian Desmond and James Moore point out in *Darwin,* 'There were simply too many plaudits, too much weighty discussion for such silly jibes to matter'. The journals were choked with Darwinism and religion/morals/philosophy - and Charles Darwin himself devoured them all.

Now with his main work behind him, Darwin's health improved. He was awarded a special degree by Cambridge University. He continued to write books - about insect eating plants, about plants and how they move and about earthworms - 'nature's first gardeners'.

In his later years, Darwin attempted to sum up the qualities which had led him to produce such world shattering books. "My success as a man of science, whatever this may have amounted to, has been determined as far as I can judge, by complex and diversified mental qualities and conditions. Of these the most important have been the love of science, unbounded patience in long reflecting over any subject, industry in observing and collecting facts, and a fair share of invention as well as of common sense".

Darwin died at Downe House in Kent on April 19th 1882, of a heart attack. He and his family had always thought that he would be buried in St Mary's churchyard, Downe, along with his ancestors. But after pressure from the Royal Society and many prominent figures of the day, the family agreed that the old agnostic would be laid to rest in Westminster Abbey. The great and the good attended the funeral -

politicians, inventors, explorers, scientists, artists and members of the scientific societies of many countries. The nation, in fact the world, had at last come to terms with Charles Darwin.

Swashbuckling Founder of First New World Colony

SIR HUMPHREY GILBERT (1539-1583)

If asked about famous Elizabethan merchant adventurers (or 'swashbuckling pirates' if you prefer) then most people would come up with the likes of Sir Walter Raleigh, Sir Francis Drake and Sir John Hawkins. But there is a fourth, with a strong Kent connection by marriage, who did much to put Britain on the map, quite literally. This man was the first Englishman to found a colony overseas, in the New World, and so, in effect, he began the process of empire building which was to culminate in the 19th century when about a third of the world was coloured red on the map, forming part of the greatest empire there had ever been.

Humphrey Gilbert was born into a wealthy family who had an estate overlooking the tidal estuary of the River Dart in Devon. He was the second son of Otho and Katherine Gilbert. His father died when he was eight and his mother remarried, the second time to Sir Walter Raleigh of Fardell in Devon; by this man she had two more sons, Walter and Carew, and a daughter Margaret. Walter was Humphrey's half-brother and it was this Walter Raleigh who went on to become famous, receiving favours, including a knighthood from Queen Elizabeth I but fell from grace and was beheaded.

Thanks to privilege and wealth Humphrey was educated at Eton and Oxford, where he devoted himself to the study of

Sir Humphrey Gilbert

navigation and war. Military service beckoned and he saw action in France and Ireland where he earned a reputation for ruthlessness. He was put in charge of the province of Munster and kept the Irish chief, McCarthy More, and his follows in subjugation; his avowed philosophy when dealing with the native Irish was 'to have neither parley nor peace with any rebel, as he was convinced no conquered nation could be ruled with gentleness.'

Although Gilbert was a good servant of the monarch he wanted more challenges, more adventure and when his military commander in Ireland Sir Henry Sidney (father of Sir Philip Sydney of Penshurst) sent him to London with dispatches for the queen, he used the audience to petition her for permission to lead an expedition to seek the North West passage across the top of America to Cathay (India). The queen was not prepared to fund such an undertaking and he was sent back to Ireland and was made president of a colony of West Countrymen near Lough Foyle in Ulster. Although this colony failed, he was knighted in 1570 and he returned to England determined to succeed in another colonising venture - this time on the other side of the Atlantic.

But the problem was financing such a venture. In Elizabethan times merchant adventurers could accumulate great wealth from successful trading expeditions, or from piracy. They either did it by their own endeavours (by owning their own ships) or by getting permission from the monarch to harass her enemies - mostly French and Spanish shipping. Sir Humphrey had been elected MP for Plymouth in 1571 and seems to have caused quite a stir by his debating style. At one time he was severely rebuked for misleading the house and called 'a flatterer, a lyer and a naughtie man'; three times he tried to speak in his self-defence and three times he was denied.

Some time around this period Sir Humphrey begins his connection with Kent. He had acquired three quarters of an estate, Otterden Manor, near Doddington from Sir John Aucher and in the process had met his daughter, Anne, who was the heiress of the remainder of the estate plus other estates at Postling and Badlesmere. He proposed marriage and she accepted, and so Sir Humphrey now had considerable assets.

Over the next few years, he tried to get others to back his scheme to found a New England in the New World. One petition was presented to the queen and was titled: 'How Her Majesty might annoy the King of Spain by fitting out a fleet of warships under pretence of a voyage of discovery, and so fall upon the enemy's shipping, destroy his trade in Newfoundland and the West Indies and possess both regions.'

Unfortunately this failed to get a response but it may well have concentrated the mind of the monarch. Queen Elizabeth knew that if England was to become a world power then she would have to follow Portugal, Spain and France and establish colonies overseas.

Finally, in 1578 he was at last in a position to proceed with his plans, but only after maximising his personal stake in the venture by pledging all of his, and his wife's, major assets. On 11 June the same year Queen Elizabeth I granted his Letters Patent which authorised him to discover, occupy and possess any 'remote heathen and barbarous landes, countries and territories, not actuallie possessed of any Christian prince or people.' This was how he was going to make his fortune and for the name Sir Humphrey Gilbert to go down in history as a great adventurer, explorer and coloniser.

The summer of 1578 saw Gilbert gathering and fitting out his expeditionary fleet of seven ships. The flagship was the *Anne Aucher,* named after his wife and both his half-brothers were involved too: Walter Raleigh captained the Falcon and Carew captained the *Hope of Greenway.* They set sail, with high hopes on 19 November but off Cape Verde they were intercepted by a hostile Spanish squadron. With one ship lost, and the others having taken a severe battering, the Englishmen were forced to turn for home, bitterly disappointed.

Needless to say the failure of the expedition was a financial disaster for Gilbert and he lost credibility at court. But he did not abandon his project; he went back to Ireland on military service, hoping to save money to try again. He provided the *Anne Aucher* and two other ships to a flotilla that was assembled off the coast of Munster to blockade the coast against Spanish ships that were supplying the Irish rebels.

In 1580, Gilbert had an opportunity to get back into parliament as an MP when he was adopted by the constituency of Queensborough on the Isle of Sheppey, to fight a by-election resulting from the death of the previous member William Butler. He was successful and soon after he established another link with Sheppey when he negotiated to buy from Henry, Lord Cheyne, the manor of Minster, which included the buildings of the ancient abbey closed by order of Henry VIII at the time of the Dissolution. The noble lord was a notorious spendthrift and had sold off extensive properties on Sheppey to pay for his lavish lifestyle and the manor was the last to go. Gilbert took possession on February 1st 1581 and soon he had moved into the Gatehouse of the Minster with his wife and five sons and one daughter.

If Lady Gilbert had hoped that now that they could enjoy a period of domestic stability after losing her inherited properties when her husband's expedition failed, she was mistaken. Sir Gilbert saw Minster Abbey as a way to raise money for another expedition and immediately began, using the expression of the day to 'pluck down' the venerable buildings - in other words, dismantling and selling as building materials the imported Caen stone, roof timbers and lead that had been used to construct the buildings that served the abbey. Eventually only the Gatehouse (the family home) and the church, used as parish place of worship, remained along with one small chapel attached, the ancient mortuary chapel of the Cheyne family. Sir Gilbert, desperate for funds, applied to the Archbishop of Canterbury to move the mortal remains of the Cheynes from the chapel to the main church. Archbishop Edmund Grindal saw fit to agree to this request, so the coffins were moved and the chapel dismantled as well and taken away in carts for use as building material elsewhere on the island.

But money was still short and he was obliged to write to the Queen's Secretary, Sir Francis Walsingham, begging to be paid for the use of his three ships against the Spanish in Ireland. He said he was reduced to poverty: 'A miserable thing it ys, having served her Majestie in warres, and peace, above seven and twenty year that I should nowe subject to daily arestes, executions, and owtlawreis; yea and forside to gadge (pawn) and sell my wyffes clothes from her back.'

Towards the end of 1581 Sir Gilbert put his last major asset on the market, the manor of Minster. Sir Edward Hobby agreed to buy it but was not forthcoming in paying the whole amount, so Sir Gilbert added a clause to his will that gave some security to the family, in that they could continue to live in the Gatehouse and receive rental income from the manor lands until such time as Sir Edward had paid the whole amount.

By the device of farming out to various parties concessions from the privileges contained in his Letters Patent, Sir Gilbert had at last got sufficient funds in hand to begin assembling another fleet to sail to America. On 11 June 1583, the expedition left Cawset Bay in Plymouth Sound. There were five ships: *Delight, Raleigh* (furnished by his half brother Walter but the queen had forbidden him to go himself), *Golden Hind, Swallow* and *Squirrel*. It must have been an ominous sign when, after only two days at sea, the largest ship with most supplies, *Raleigh,* had to turn back as a mystery illness had laid low the captain and most of the crew.

The sailing conditions were not easy but they persevered, although fog, contrary winds and icebergs delayed them. *Swallow* and *Squirrel* got separated but Sir Gilbert continued until at length land came in sight, but it was a barren, unfriendly coast. 'Nothing but hideous rocks and mountains bare of trees, and void of any green herbs' is how Edward Hayes, captain of the *Golden Hind* described it when he later wrote the account of the expedition. They turned south and sailed on and were over joyed to come across first the *Swallow* and then *Squirrel*. The crewmembers let out great cheers and threw their hats in the air to celebrate.

The four ships continued south and then sailed into the fine, almost land-locked deepwater harbour of St John's which had been used for a number of years by European boats which had come to fish the Newfoundland Banks for cod and other fish in the summer months. Sir Gilbert was about to fulfil his dream. On August 3rd 1583 he landed and solemnly took possession of the country for two hundred leagues north, south, east and west in the name of Queen Elizabeth. First his commission was read aloud and interpreted to the assorted French, Spanish and Portuguese present. Then one of the expedition brought Sir Humphrey a twig of a hazel tree and a sod of earth and put them in his hands, as a sign that he took possession of the land and all that was in it. Finally the arms of England engraved on lead was fixed to a wooden pillar and after a prayer to God, the ceremony was completed.

Straight away the colony was in trouble. Members of the expedition had included shipwrights, masons, carpenters, smiths, mineral men and refiners and they should have set about establishing the colony. But Sir Gilbert seems to have been an excellent planner but not a very good leader of men. Hayes observed that 'amongst a multitude of voluntary men, their dispositions were diverse, which bred a jar, and made a division in the end, to the confusion of that attempt even before the same was begun.'

Some men deserted and secured passage back to Europe on other ships. Others went off into the forest and hid, hoping to escape work while another group mutinied, forcibly took over a French fishing boat, made the crew go ashore after stealing their clothes, and then sailed out of the harbour and headed back to England. But others went about their work, including one of the refiners, whose job it was to look for minerals. His name was Daniel and he reported a find, with a sample, of what was probably iron ore. The leader was very excited by this as part of the reason for the expedition was to look for ways to make the colony economic and with iron ore present you could make all manner of tools and building materials.

With defections, sickness and even deaths, there were not enough crew to man four ships; so leaving all the sick and a few colonists who wished to remain with the *Swallow*, Sir Gilbert was keen to explore further south. They had a consignment of 'petty haberdashery wares' with which they would barter with the natives and they also had a number of musical instruments with which to entertain them as well as toys, like 'morris dancers, hobby-horse and May-like conceits to delight the savage, people whom we intended to win by all fair means possible.'

But their ill luck continued - storms and fog made it impossible to get in close to shore even though Sir Gilbert had pointedly made the smallest, and most manoeuvrable ship the *Squirrel* his flagship. Disaster struck when the *Delight* went aground and broke up - all of Sir Gilbert's books and notes were aboard that boat, along with the precious sample of the mineral, and he was devastated by losing them as well as about 100 men presumed drowned. In fact, he did not know about his books and notes until later - he had told his cabin boy to take them aboard the *Squirrel* but he had forgotten to carry out the order. When Sir Gilbert found that out he flew into a terrible rage and beat him horribly. In fact, 14 men from the *Delight* had survived miraculously; they had abandoned ship for a small eight oared pinnace and eventually made it back to St John's, an extraordinary brave act of seamanship in such foul weather which took six days, although two died on route.

Sir Gilbert did not want to abandon his men as some might be alive - so he sailed up and down the coast in terrible weather trying to get in close where the ship had foundered but was always beaten back. Morale was at an all time low, and after several petitions and pleadings from his wet and miserable men, he agreed to set sail for England on condition that they would return in the following spring.

The *Squirrel* was the smallest of the two ships and the captain of the *Golden Hind* wanted to get the expedition leader to come on board his ship, for his own safety. Sir Gilbert refused, saying he'd got to know his ship mates well over the weeks and months and had 'past through many storms and perils with them.' It was a fateful decision.

Although the wind was in their favour the seas were huge and the little ship was in danger of being engulfed, as it rose to the top of each giant swell and then plunged into the trough. At night lights were set so they could keep in touch with each other. The last that was seen of Sir Gilbert was one afternoon in September when the two ships were close enough for the leader to shout across to the *Golden Hind:* "We are as near to heaven by sea as by land." He had been in the prow of the ship reading a book.

Then the sun went down and darkness fell over the wild sea. One minute the lights of the *Squirrel* could be seen, the next they had disappeared. Immediately the watch called out that the frigate was lost. As Master Hayes recorded: 'it was too true. For in that moment the frigate was devoured and swallowed up by the sea.'

The *Golden Hind* made it safely back to England and the survivors reported on the ill-fated expedition. Sir Gilbert's widow and family were forced to leave Minster and go and live with family in Hollingbourne. Sir Edward Hobby appeared in no hurry to discharge his debt to her but Lady Anne had friends at court in Sir John Walsingham and Sir Walter Raleigh, who appealed to the queen on her behalf. In June 1585, her financial plight was eased considerably when the Crown confiscated lands belonging to a Richard Guilford in Kent and gave them to her. And Sir Edward Hobby did eventually pay her for the manor at Minster, which may have been some compensation for the loss of her brave, if unlucky husband.

Man Of A Thousand Novels

CHARLES HAROLD ST JOHN HAMILTON (1876-1961)

Charles Hamilton was probably the most prolific writer who ever lived, something that is recorded in the *Guinness Book of Records.* For most of his writing career, he wrote at least six stories and serials a week under about 20 different pen-names and sent off some 60 replies to fan letters. When pushed, he could produce as many as 18,000 words in a single day. So, based on an annual output of more than 1,500,000 words, it is reckoned that he had a lifetime output of more than 100,000,000 words which is the rough equivalent of some 1,000 ordinary novels.

Hamilton's most famous pen name was Frank Richards, creator of Greyfriars School and Billy Bunter - the Fat Owl of the Remove, the prevaricating tuck-hunter forever waiting for a postal order that never came. To some, Bunter is literature's most famous school boy, along with Tom Brown. The difference of course is that Tom Brown's life was tinged with sadness, Bunter's outrageous behaviour brought only tears of laughter.

Hamilton became a Kent man in 1925, when he moved into Rose Lawn in Percy Avenue, Kingsgate-on-Sea, Broadstairs - where he spent the rest of his life. He loved both the country and the sea and here he had the best of both.

He was born at 15 Oak Street, Ealing, on August 8th 1876 and was sixth in a family of five brothers and three sisters. His birth certificate states that his father was a carpenter but the *Dictionary of National Biography* insists that this is not true: that his father was in fact a journalist and sometime bookseller and stationer. He died when Charles was seven, after which the family moved house frequently.

Hamilton's biographers complain that in his *Autobiography of Frank Richards,* the author is very reticent about his childhood. However, we do know that he was a keen reader from an early age, was educated privately and also attended a Private School for Young Gentlemen - Thorne House School, Ealing. Charles's education left him with a good knowledge of French and Latin and a love of the classics.

He later wrote a Bunter story in Latin and translated several popular songs into the language. A gossip columnist rang to have this confirmed; in response, Charles broke into song with a Latin rendition of *The Man Who Broke the Bank at Monte Carlo.* The BBC heard about it and three broadcasts followed.

Charles wrote his first short story in 1885 and sold his first piece when he was only 17. He received a cheque for five guineas from a 'Mr M', who reduced future payments to four pounds when he discovered the budding author's young age. Charles sold further stories with ease, concentrating on boys' papers.

In 1907 the Amalgamated Press launched *Gem,* followed a year later by *Magnet.* Hamilton became a regular contributor to both for the next 30 years - the lifetime of the magazines. At the same time, he contributed to

Charles Hamilton

other publications, using various pseudonyms. As well as boys' stories, he also wrote westerns, adventure, romance, travel, crime, science-fiction, humour and serious yarns. He even worked on a translation of Horace's odes.

The first Bunter story rolled off his No 7 Remington in 1908. Asked how his favourite character originated, the author said that Bunter was the combination of several people. 'His circumstance was that of an editor I knew who overflowed his chair; his long-awaited postal order was originally a cheque which a friend of mine was constantly expecting'.

In the *Gem,* as Martin Clifford, he invented a school called St Jim's. In other plots, he wrote of as many as 100 imaginary schools. But his real favourite was his creation in the *Magnet.* Greyfriars and company were to make Frank Richards a household name and it was by this name that he preferred to be called. It is said that only his bank manager called him Charles Hamilton. At one time, it was reckoned that, after Shakespeare, he was the most often quoted author - in papers ranging from *The Times* to the *Sun*.

'The Famous Five' consisted of Harry Wharton (Captain of the Remove), Johnny Bull, the down-to-earth Yorkshire boy, Hurree Jamset Ram Singh (His Royal Highness the Nabob of Bhanipur), Bob Cherry and Frank Nugent. There were 23 other boys in the form including Bunter. But these were just the core characters. McCall's *Greyfriars Guide* identifies over 3,000 people and places in 1,000 issues of the *Magnet*. Altogether, he created about 5,000 stories. More than 3,111 were reprinted into various other publications.

Despite this enormous success, Frank Richards was not without his critics. George Orwell among others said that the writing was atrocious and out of date and that the characters were goodie-goodie and stereotyped. The stories were wholly escapist, nurtured snobbishness, and represented foreigners as funny.

Hamilton replied that aristocratic virtues were worth preserving and that foreigners *were* funny. As for the stories being escapist, this surely was the whole point of the exercise. The world of Greyfriars never did exist outside the author's imagination, even in 1907. In the tailpiece to Maurice Hall's biography *I Say, You Fellows!,* Chris Lowder sums up the author's enigmatic character.

When you get right down to it, Lowder says, for the last 30 years of his life, Hamilton was completely out of touch with reality. (He cites an example of crooks using a horse-drawn caravan as a getaway vehicle in 1960!) Utterly immersed in his stories, to him his fictional world became more real than the real world.

But all this didn't really matter. Hamilton told superb yarns and his characters were true to form within the context of the story. He was true to his ideals, he was funny and he took some marvellous swipes at politicians, the *nouveau riche,* and the law - among many other targets of his astringent wit.

Perhaps the critics were right when they said he couldn't write about real people. Instead, Lowder maintains, he injected wonderful reality into unreal people.

And above all, he provided escape. He invited you into a pretend world where, though there might be dark clouds, the sun always shone through in the end. For a while we can enter his world in the happy anticipation of pleasures to be savoured and cherished. To be always 12, always secure. The reader comes out of it refreshed. And if Hamilton could do that, he had achieved a very great deal.

Hamilton used a similar argument to defend the fact that sex never entered the adolescent world of Greyfriars or elsewhere in his creations. It is an argument that would get him nowhere in the know-all nowadays. He felt that the less the young person thought about sex, the better. 'I am aware that in these modern days, there are people who think their children should be told things which, in my own childhood, no small person was allowed to hear ... my own opinion is that such people suffer from disordered digestions which cause their minds to take a nasty turn. They fancy they are realists when they are only obscene. The go grubbing in the sewers for their realism'.

Hamilton was fully convinced that his job as a writer was to take people out of themselves. One day in real life a lad may search for a job - and not get it. On another day he might get the sack. Why tell him about it at 12? ... Every day of happiness, illusory or otherwise - and most happiness is illusory - is much to the good and worth having'. There were always masses of readers to agree with him. John Major and Frederick Forsyth are among his greatest fans.

The outbreak of war put an end to the *Gem* in 1939 and to the *Magnet* in 1940. Hamilton's earnings at the time were upwards of £2,500 a year, then a substantial sum. But he had also spent freely, so the demise of two of his best earners was a heavy blow.

His time came again with the post-war mood of nostalgia. Billy Bunter began appearing between hard covers, of which more than 30 were published. Then in 1952, Hamilton wrote Bunter scripts for television and Bunter Christmas shows were staged in London. Now in his late seventies, he was the oldest scriptwriter in the business. Fame, however, did not affect him and visitors to his bungalow at Kingsgate-on-Sea found an old fashioned, reserved figure in a black skull-cap, dressing gown, and trousers cycle-clipped against the cold. When relaxing, he would take his cat Sammy on his knee and listen to classical music, his pipe seldom out of his mouth.

As he grew older, Hamilton's eyesight began to fail him. 'Today, my world ends at the garden gate', he told a friend. Despite this, he never failed to answer the constant stream of letters that came from old and new readers. Ideas for Bunter stories kept flowing but his output suffered. Despite that, he still wrote some 250,000 words a year - better than most young writers - achieved from a working day of 9 am to midday! He died at the age of 86 - in his sleep on Christmas Eve 1961.

✳ ✳ ✳

Discovered Circulation of Blood

WILLIAM HARVEY (1578-1657)

William Harvey proved what had been suspected for centuries - that blood was circulated one way around the body by arteries and veins, being taken to and from the lungs where it got oxygen, by the pumping action of the heart. Even the founders of medicine like Aristotle and Galen suspected that this was the case, but the Folkestone-born doctor used sound scientific study to confirm it. In fact Harvey deserves to be up there in the top rank with the likes of Newton, Darwin and Einstein - all scientists who created a new epoch in human knowledge.

William's parents were from solid Kent stock. His father Thomas was a yeoman farmer with land at Burmarsh on Romney Marsh. He was also a business man and merchant and had a house (later the post house in Mercery Lane, now Church Street) in Folkestone. He was also an alderman and four times mayor of the town. Thomas married Joane, the daughter of Thomas Halke of Hastingleigh in Kent; it was the second marriage for him. Their first child was a daughter and then William was born, 'the first of a week of sons' according to a contemporary writer.

At the age of ten, William was sent to boarding school in Canterbury, to the King's School attached to the cathedral, where he got a good grounding in Greek and Latin, the language that he would use

William Harvey

in later life to write the books that would make his name. In 1593 he went to Gonville and Caius College, Cambridge as a commoner but was soon awarded the Matthew Parker scholarship for the study of medicine. His studies were disrupted for the best part of a year by illness - probably malaria - but he was awarded a BA in 1597.

Harvey was determined to continue his medical studies and proceeded to the University of Padua, which was reputed to be the best school of medicine in Europe. For two and a half years he studied under the guidance of a celebrated anatomist and teacher, Hieronymus Fabricus ab Aquapendente. It was in the now-famous wood panelled oval Anatomy Theatre, still to be seen at the university, that Harvey first recognised the problems posed by the function of the beating heart and the properties of the blood passing through it.

He was a diligent and popular student and was elected Conciliarius, or leader of the English students at Padua. One of his contemporaries described his engaging personality, a bonus in a doctor who needs a rapport with his patient, and testified 'to the great goodwill, the esteem and devotion he excited among those around him, for such was his nature.'

There is a brief description of him as a student: 'he was rather on the small side, with raven hair, dark piercing eyes, somewhat sallow complexion, and keen restless demeanour and rapid speech. He was a keen and accurate observer and an enthusiastic naturalist, and he had a mind reflective as to the causes and relations of things.'

He became a Doctor of Medicine in 1602 and, returning to Cambridge took his MD there and began to practice in London where he quickly began to make a reputation for himself and his career took off. He was admitted to the College of Physicians in April 1604 and married Elizabeth Browne, the daughter of a physician, in the following November. But his father-in-law was not just any physician, but Lancelot Browne, doctor to King James I and his queen, and a senior fellow of the college. Such connections did the young physician no harm: in 1607 he was elected Fellow of the College, followed two years later by Physician to St Bartholomew's Hospital and Lumleian Lecturer at the College in 1616.

St Bart's at that time had about 200 beds in 12 wards and his duties consisted of attending on at least one day a week in the main hall with patients who could walk coming to see him and sitting at the main table in front of a great fireplace, the fire of which was kept going by a supply of wood from the forest of Windsor, a privilege given to the hospital by Henry III. He received an annual salary of £25 with £2 extra for his livery and £8 in lieu of not living in the official physician's residence on site (he lived with his wife just nearby in St Martin's). Harvey held this office for 34 years, when he was displaced, for political reasons by Oliver Cromwell's regime, which held sway in London and disliked his royal connections.

As for his lecturing at the College of Physicians, he was expected to use real corpses when demonstrating the organs and functions of the body. This could be something of a problem, especially in summer when they quickly putrefied. Harvey developed a series of three lectures which could be delivered in about an hour for each. The first looked at the outside of the body, the second with the chest and its contents and the third was on the head, including the brains and nerves. He was always cutting up bodies of animals to increase his knowledge of anatomy and had the king's permission to use deer killed in the chase from the royal park at Windsor. He was particularly pleased when an injured animal was brought to him as the technique of vivisection could be used to give him the evidence that he needed to prove his theories on blood circulation.

Harvey had been telling his students about circulation for some 12 years but it was only when he published his findings that the medical profession took notice. The book was published in Frankfurt by William Fitzer in 1628. Written in Latin it was quarto in size, 72 pages with two plates of diagrams. Entitled *Exercitatio Anatomica de Motu Cordis et Sanguinis in Animalibus* (On the Motion of the Heart and Blood in Animals), it remains to this day the greatest of the discoveries of physiology.

Needless to say, there were some in the medical profession, especially on the Continent, who disputed his discovery and dismissed him as 'crackbrained'; for a time he feared injury to himself from the envy of others. But he patiently and good naturedly would argue his case, and all the time his reputation was increasing as well as his wealth as more and more people wanted to be treated by the eminent physician. In 1618 he was appointed physician-extraordinary to James I and was called upon, when the king died, to defend the reputation of the monarch's favourite, the Duke of Buckingham, who was actually accused of having poisoned the king. Harvey's testimony exonerated the duke.

Charles I continued the doctor's royal appointment as his personal physician and the two became good friends. Whenever the king travelled he would go with him - on one state visit to Scotland, Harvey used the opportunity to visit the Bass Rock to study the colony of breeding gannets. He was a keen naturalist and wrote up accounts of his observations. Whenever he could he would cut up a bird or animal to see how the internal organs were arranged; he performed this task on over 60 different species during his lifetime.

In 1634 four Lancashire women were accused of witchcraft and Harvey was asked to lead the examining group consisting of ten midwives and seven surgeons. They found there was nothing unnatural in their bodies and so they were pardoned. The following year he gave a tanned human skin to the College of Physicians 'for a monument to be reserved'. He was not above reproach for one 'impudent barber surgeon' claimed Harvey was responsible for malpractice on a maidservant, which lead to her death. He defended himself rigorously and his reputation remained intact. Another celebrated case for him was the post-mortem of a Shropshire labourer, Thomas Parr, who was supposed to have lived 152 years and nine months.

As personal doctor to the king, Harvey was present at the battle of Edgehill. But he seems to have been little interested in the politics and drama of the Civil War. As the king's army was assembling Harvey went to Derby to visit a doctor friend, Percival Willughby, and they talked about uterine diseases and as the battle itself raged, he read a book in the company of the two princes, Wales and the Duke of York. Harvey followed the king to Oxford and was appointed Warden of Merton College. At the university he devoted himself to further experiments in embryology by studying the development of chicks in hens' eggs. He was very interested in fertility, possibly because he and his wife had had no children. While at Oxford and in attendance to the king, Harvey could not carry out any duties or researches in London, which was a Parliamentarian stronghold. He was bitterly disappointed to learn that a mob had attacked his apartment in Whitehall and ransacked it, burning all his books and notes relevant to his medical work and experiments.

In 1645 his wife died and the following year, after the surrender of Oxford, he fled north with the king who gave himself up to the Scots. In January 1647 the king was handed over to the forces of Oliver Cromwell and Harvey was told his services were no longer required. The doctor was allowed to go back to London where he lodged in one or other of his brothers' houses in the surrounding countryside; they had become rich and were successful merchants. Charles I was put on trial, but the king's refusal to plead was taken by the court as a confession to being a traitor, tyrant and murderer and he was beheaded on January 30th 1649. Harvey was a broken and unhappy man by this time, and regarded as a 'political delinquent' owing to his long association with the royal family. He virtually gave up practicing medicine, but continued to do some research into reproduction.

His second great book *Exercitatio Anatomica de Generatione Animalium* (Anatomical Exercitations, Concerning the Generation of Living Creatures) was published in 1653. With the chapter on midwifery, he founded the study of gynaecology, as it was the first work on the subject to be written by an Englishman.

Harvey's greatness as a scientist and as a thinker was recognised by his fellows in the College of Physicians who elected him as their President in 1654. However he declined the honour on account of old age and infirmity. He suffered from kidney stones and attacks of gout, which he would treat by sitting with his feet in cold water. He described himself to a friend in a letter that he was 'not only ripe in years, but also a little weary and entitled to an honourable discharge.' He had already generously built a Hall and Library for the college and given it his collection of medical books - unfortunately all of this was destroyed in the Great Fire of London in 1666.

When he died in 1657 there were a number of bequests in his will. He left his father's farm on Romney Marsh to the College of Physicians and the family home in Folkestone to his Cambridge College, Gonville and Caius. He wanted his brother Eliab to have his coffee pot. There was also £200 for the poor of his native town. Part of this money went to found a Free School in Folkestone, which today is the Harvey Grammar School.

Liked to be in a Minority of One

WILLIAM HAZLITT (1778-1830)

Maidstone's principal theatre is named after a writer and critic often described as 'a flawed genius'. William Hazlitt had such a difficult character - fastidious, petty, spiteful - that family and friends despaired of him but it is in his original thinking and facility with wit and words that his reputation was secured. He positively delighted in being in a minority of one to the extent that his dying words were supposed to have been: "Well, I've had a happy life." Many who knew him must have surely thought: "Well, you could have fooled me."

William was born in Mitre Lane, Maidstone on April 10th 1778, the third child of the Minister in the Unitarian Church, which still stands close to the theatre. His father was also called William and he had studied at Glasgow for five years where he was a contemporary of the economist and philosopher Adam Smith. William senior joined the Presbyterian ministry and then become a Unitarian and had been a minister in Wisbeach (where he met and married farmer's daughter Grace Loftus) and Marshfield, Gloucester before moving to Maidstone in 1770.

The Hazlitt family sailed for America in 1783 when William was five and his father preached in Philadelphia and gave lectures in the college there of the evidence of Christianity. He also founded the first Unitarian church in Boston. It must have been an exciting time for the young boy in the newly independent colonies and the experience shaped his thinking; family letters of the time were already indicating a precocious intellect.

The family was back in England in 1787 and when he was 15 William was sent to the Unitarian college in Hackney to prepare for the ministry. Just a year before, in 1792, he had already written and had published *A Project for a New Theory of Criminal and Civil Legislation,* so this was no ordinary teenager. For some reason Hazlitt did not complete his studies and so forfeited the chance of becoming a church minister. But he was moving in the right circles for becoming a literary figure. He got to know Coleridge when the poet came to preach at his father's church and through him he met Wordsworth. (Later in one of his lectures on English poets he said about Coleridge: "He talked on for ever; and you wished him to talk on for ever.")

After giving up college William went to live with his father where he continued his studies by reading philosophical writers like Burke, Junius and Rousseau as well as novels and other works by Fielding, Smollett and Richardson. He was quite candid about the many blanks in his reading and though he may have thought about reading the Greek and German classics he never bothered. He is said never to have read a book through to the end after the age of 30.

His delight in solitary thought made him a gauche and furtive figure at social gatherings, being very ill at ease in company. He would sit on the edge of his chair having dropped his hat on the floor, with his chin on his walking stick, and mutter to himself. If not interested in the talk he would leave brusquely cursing the idiot company.

William's elder brother John was a successful miniature painter and for a time he thought he could earn a living at that too. He spent four months in Paris over the winter of 1802-3, making copies of paintings at the Louvre, for which he had several commissions from his friends (his painting of Charles Lamb as a Venetian senator hangs in the National Portrait Gallery). Back in London, he wrote learned, but dry, accounts about ethics and philosophical issues and the Lambs added him to their literary milieu.

William Hazlitt

Now in his late twenties, the moody writer with a pale complexion that was made more pallid by a shock of wavy black hair was falling in and out of love quite regularly. He seems to have put some women off by his actions and others were not allowed to go out with him when their fathers or guardians saw him. On one occasion he was thrown into a stream when his advances went too far.

In 1808 Hazlitt married a Miss Sarah Stodhart who had inherited some country property near Salisbury, which produced an annual income of

£120. She was a ward of her brother, as their father had died and their mother was insane. The brother was none too pleased with her sister's choice but she was no longer young nor pretty and had suffered a string of broken romances. The matchmaker had been one of Hazlitt's literary circle, Mary Lamb, who was also a bridesmaid at their wedding in St Andrew's Church in Holborn.

Hazlitt could hardly have endeared himself to his wife-to-be when he wrote just before the marriage: 'I never love you so well as when I think of sitting down with you to dinner over a boiled scragg-end of mutton and hot potatoes.' They lived in a country cottage on his father's estate and Hazlitt concentrated on his writing. Their first-born son died in infancy but a second, named William, appeared on September 26th 1811. The following year they moved to London in order to be nearer literary employment. As well as writing for the likes of *London Magazine* and *The Times,* Hazlitt also gave lectures on modern philosophy.

Hazlitt's journalism took a new direction when he became a parliamentary correspondent for the *Morning Chronicle,* where his wit and facility to write sketches came to the fore. From simply reporting debates, he began to write commentaries on them, and his work was both admired and appreciated. His style was biting and crystal clear and he feared no one, nor any party. His comment on the Whig and Tory parties was that they were like rival stagecoaches, splashing each other with mud as they rattled along, but both arriving at the same destination.

If he upset his friends and family, then he also upset the Establishment. He was an enthusiastic supporter of the French Revolution and his hero was Napoleon. He spent the last years of his life writing a *Life of Napoleon* and was originally drawn to him because the Corsican-born Frenchman represented antagonism to the doctrine of the divine right of kings.

Like many a journalist since, drinking became very much part of his working life, but it was never 'just the one' after work to unwind. In 1815, after a long drinking bout intended to drown the memory of Napoleon's defeat at Waterloo, his doctor warned him that the drink would kill him if he did not give up. From that point the drunkard became an ex-drunkard and strong black tea quaffed in Johnsonian quantities became his only tipple.

From being a political writer, he turned his attention to dramatic and literary criticism, and a stream of brilliant essays and commentaries flowed from his pen. In 1817 he published *Characters from Shakespeare's Plays* and then followed *View of the English Stage* and then *English Comic*

Writers. Editors loved Hazlitt for his words, if not for himself, as he could write sublimely on any subject whether literary, political, artistic or dramatic.

As well as playing a large part in shaping the thinking of the early 19th century, much of his prose is still very readable today. Most anthologies have Hazlitt quotes. 'If the world were good for nothing else, it is a fine subject for speculation.' 'The least pain in our little finger gives us more concern and uneasiness than the destruction of millions of our fellow-beings.' 'His worst is better than any other person's best.' (about Sir Walter Scott). 'His sayings are generally like women's letters; all the pith is in the postscript' (about Charles Lamb). 'A nickname is the heaviest stone that the devil can throw at a man.' 'The English (it must be owned) are rather a foul-mouthed race.' 'When I am in the country I wish to vegetate like the country.' 'Rules and models destroy genius and art.'

But on the domestic front things were not going well. Sarah had left him in 1819 and three years later they were divorced. The celebrated critic does not seem to be self critical: 'Even in the common affairs of life,' he wrote, 'in love, friendship and marriage, how little security have we when we trust our happiness in the hands of others.'

After his wife left him, Hazlitt took lodgings with a tailor named Walker in Soho who had a pretty 20-year-old daughter, also named Sarah. He became infatuated with her to the point of obsession saying that Providence had sent her as a consolation for Napoleon's defeat at Waterloo. If that was the case then Providence had not told Sarah. Despite every artifice and blandishment - 'vestal virgin, little idol, young witch with serpent arms, phantom of delight, demon destroyer' - she was underwhelmed by the attentions of the man over twice her age.

He convinced himself that it was her stubborn virtuousness which was driving him to distraction, and in an attempt to break the spell she had cast on him, he wrote to those friends he thought that he could trust. He urged them to try and seduce her, praying that they might succeed where he had failed, and in doing so rid him of his obsession with her. 'If only I knew she was a whore,' he wrote, 'it would wean me from her, and burst my chain!' Hazlitt even paid an agent, 'Mr F', to take lodgings with the Walkers (he had had to move out by then) and lay siege to Sarah's chastity.

When all this failed he published all his letters to Sarah and to his friends and to Mr F detailing the planned seduction in a book *Liber Amoris*. It was universally condemned, with the magazine *John Bull* pulling no punches describing it 'as Billy Hazlitt's nasty book' and his attempts to 'degrade a very pretty and innocent girl'. But he never forgot

Sarah and his thoughts were of her, even on his deathbed.

Possibly to try and forget Sarah, Hazlitt met and married a pretty young widower in April 1824. Isabella Bridgewater had gone out to the West Indies with her husband, a planter, but he had died of a fever and she had returned to England with an income of £300 per year. This was used by the couple to travel on the continent for a year but then strains began to appear. Hazlitt's son, William, was 13 at this time and he hated his pretty young stepmother. The father adored his son and so was put in an impossible situation. His difficult character did not help the relationship and, of course, there was the difference in age, with his wife still in her twenties and he was in his forties. Isabella left her husband after three years and Hazlitt spent the rest of his life alone.

His bitterness was real when the biography of his hero Napoleon failed to achieve literary success. He wrote; 'There is not a more mean, stupid, dastardly, pitiful, selfish, spiteful, envious, ungrateful animal than the public. It is the greatest of cowards, for it is afraid of itself.'

His health began to fail and perhaps he felt that after life's ultimate experience he might achieve some recognition of his last literary work. He wrote: 'When a man is dead, they put money in his coffin, erect monuments to his memory, and celebrate the anniversary of his birth in set speeches. Would they take any notice of him if he were alive? No!' Such an outpouring makes his dying words even more puzzling.

Hazlitt died of stomach cancer on September 18th 1830 and is buried in St Anne's Churchyard in Soho.

Dean with Heartening Courage or Deluded?

DR HEWLETT JOHNSON (1874-1966)

Dr Hewlett Johnson

Canterbury seems to have a tradition of controversial church ministers which goes back to the most famous of all, Thomas à Becket, described by Henry II somewhat impetuously as 'this turbulent priest'. Becket was Archbishop and murdered by four of the king's knights; Dr Hewlett Johnson was merely the Dean but caused such consternation in the Establishment with his support of Communism that many would have cheerfully throttled him. In the event, the so-called 'Red Dean' stepped down but not before spending decades upsetting people both at home and abroad with his political views.

Born on January 25th 1874 in Manchester, Hewlett was the third son of Charles Johnson, a wire manufacturer and his wife Rosa. He got his unusual Christian name from his mother's side of the family, as it was her maiden name. Possibly he got more than a name from his maternal side as his grandfather was Reverend Alfred Hewlett, who worked in the parish of Astley for more than 50 years where he was known as the 'Spurgeon of the North' (Charles Haddon Spurgeon 1834 - 1892 was considered a great preacher).

He was educated at Macclesfield Grammar School and the Owens College, Manchester where he gained a B Sc in 1894 and was awarded the geological prize. In 1898 he became an associate member of the Institute of Civil Engineers and it seemed he was destined for a career in business or commerce. But his knowledge of the slums of Manchester combined with a religious upbringing pointed him in the direction of a religious vocation and he offered his services to the Church Missionary Society. To begin his religious studies, he went to Wadham College, Oxford and got a second class BA honours degree in theology to go with his science degree.

But even then he was getting a reputation for outspokenness and his radical views made him unacceptable for the CMS. But the Church of England is a broad church and he was appointed a curate in the parish of St Margaret, Altrincham in 1904. He quickly rose 'through the ranks' - deacon 1905, priest 1906, vicar 1909, honorary canon of Chester 1919, rural dean of Bowden 1922 and in that same year his fellow clergy elected him a proctor in Convocation, the Church's ruling body or synod.

Johnson was very popular among the 'rank and file' of his congregation, even if some of the wealthy industrialists of the North did not appreciate his developing views on socialism. Whilst carrying out his parish work, he also found time to edit a theological magazine - *The Interpreter* - to which many leading scholars of the day contributed. When he wasn't editing, he was studying, taking a Batchelor of Divinity from Oxford in 1917 followed by a doctorate in 1924 with his thesis on the Acts of the Apostles.

In the same year that he was awarded his Doctor of Divinity he was appointed to the deanery of Manchester. He possessed many of the qualities looked for in a dean: he preached well; he looked every inch a dignitary of the Church as he was tall and wore gaiters, the proper dress for deans at that time, and, of course a dog collar; he was keenly interested in civic affairs and he had considerable charm. He was also involved in secular activities. Once he had to judge some costermongers' donkeys and a photo duly appeared in the *Guardian,* with the caption; 'The Dean with the donkeys - the Dean can be distinguished by his silk hat.' And he also had a Mancunian wife; he had married Mary, daughter of Frederick Taylor, a successful merchant, in 1903 and she was very much liked too in her home city. Mary died in 1931 and that same year he moved to the deanery of Canterbury.

At the time of his appointment to Canterbury, Johnson's politics were not clear-cut. He was interested in industrial conditions; he deplored the massive unemployment; he felt the government should do more to ease economic inequalities. But he was not, as yet, 'red'.

The dean liked to travel - he claimed to have visited all the cathedrals in Europe - but he did not find his way to Russia until 1937. The rise of Fascism in Germany and Italy and his outspoken support of the Republican government in Spain had already predisposed him in favour of the Soviet experiment. When he observed it at first hand, he was completely captivated. Surprisingly for a man familiar with research and scholarship, and used to testing theories in debate, he refused to see any wrong in a system that he considered was helping the cause of human betterment.

He not only spoke up for the Soviet achievements, he wrote about them as well. In what amounted to a eulogy, Johnson's book *The Socialist Sixth of the World* was a publishing phenomenon in 1939. The Red Dean had expected to sell a few hundred copies but, in fact, it went on to sell several million reaching 22 editions in 24 languages. Its publication caused a furore. It so infuriated his colleagues at Canterbury that they wrote to *The Times* dissociating themselves from his political utterances and expressing the view that his political activities gravely impaired the spiritual influence of the Cathedral in the City and Diocese of Canterbury. One of the signatories, Canon Crum, formerly a good friend, refused to sit with the Dean in Chapter and would not partake of communion if he was there.

Even though Johnson was upsetting his former friends, there was no doubting his commitment to the people of Canterbury, who were very much in the front line, once France had fallen and air raids on London and other targets began. The worst night was to come on June 1st 1942 in the so-called Baedecker Raid by the Luftwaffe. Two nights before the RAF had virtually obliterated Cologne and in retaliation targets in England had been selected by consulting the famous travel guide. Lord Haw Haw announced chillingly that Canterbury was to be a target.

The planes arrived over Canterbury in the early hours and released wave after wave of bombs and some 6,000 incendiary devices, causing enormous damage. Miraculously the Cathedral only received superficial damage thanks to the vigilance of the firewatchers, although other buildings in the Precinct were destroyed. Johnson and all the canons put aside their differences and worked tirelessly over the next few days, bringing comfort and relief to those who had lost loved ones or been injured.

After the war, Johnson's loyalty to the official Soviet Party line was unflinching to the point of embarrassment. He perversely held fast to what he wanted to believe and dismissed from his mind anything that might shatter his illusions - the secret trials, the terrorism, the concentration camps, the atrocities of Stalin, the invasion of Hungary. In the Cold War era, he was a godsend to the Soviets and was awarded, and accepted, the Stalin Peace Medal in 1951; they could hardly believe their good fortune in having such a high profile propagandist. Was he not the Dean of Canterbury Cathedral, the spiritual home of the Church of England?

Many people abroad, unfamiliar with the hierarchy in the Church, thought him to be the spiritual leader too, and he did not go out of his way to disabuse them of this fact. He wrote: 'I realised that Canterbury, the centre of the Anglican Communion, would be my perfect platform for world peace, and I have been able to make the world my parish. I am the Dean, so they read what I write, although they may not agree with it.' Because he travelled extensively and spoke volubly, he was very much 'high profile'. In 1947 the Archbishop of Canterbury was forced to clarify the situation with an official statement that ended: 'The Dean's office and jurisdiction in this country does not extend beyond the confines of the Cathedral body of which he is the head. Outside those limits he speaks and acts only for himself. The Archbishop of Canterbury has neither responsibility for what the Dean may say or do, nor the power to control it.'

In the early 1950s, Archbishop Fisher was asked again and again about the Red Dean; he often described him as 'a charming, gracious, friendly, pastoral man, once he was off his main subject of socialism and Russia.' On one visit to Australia and New Zealand, the Archbishop even took the trouble to have pre-printed replies to the inevitable question ready for hand out. It read: 'Doctor Johnson cannot be deprived of his position unless he breaks civil or ecclesiastical laws. He has broken no law. He has only expressed his opinions. I violently disagree with them but, as long as we have freedom of speech in England Dr Johnson will remain.' Arriving at the New York dockside in the autumn of 1952 during a thunderstorm, the Archbishop found himself shouting above it; "I am not the Red Dean! I am not the Red Dean!"

But on one occasion the Red Dean pushed the Archbishop, too far. On Easter Day 1956 George Malenkov, the recently demoted Soviet Prime Minister and the Russian Ambassador were entertained by Johnson to luncheon and tea in the deanery and were shown around the Cathedral by him personally. At one point they passed Archbishop Fisher departing in a procession at the end of a service. A little later the Dean received a furious letter from Dr Fisher for bringing 'unbelievers' into the Cathedral on Easter Day.

Johnson continued to court controversy adding China and Cuba as well as other East European Communist States to the places he visited, although he was denied a visa to the USA for his denouncement of their participation in the Korean War. He became as enthusiastic about the Peking brand of Communism as he had been about the Moscow version, although it was said that the criticism and counter-criticism of the two regimes were a cause of embarrassment to him, had he been capable by then of the same.

Despite his eloquent and forceful preaching, many acts of great personal kindness, his graciousness, his enormous pride in the upkeep and the dignity of one the greatest cultural treasures in all the world, it must have been with an enormous sense of relief from many when he finally came to resign. Scrupulous in not giving any cause for being sacked, eventually events came to a head, and as he put it 'the Canons wanted me to go - and said so, vehemently.' So he went in 1963; but it was a retirement, not a resignation nor a sacking. He was, after all, nearly 90.

He had married for the second time in 1938, Nowell Mary, daughter of his cousin, the late Reverend George Edwards; they had two daughters. Upon his retirement, Johnson and his wife wanted to stay in Canterbury and they moved to a house in St Dunstan's called 'Orchard Villa'. With an impish sense of humour, he wanted to rename it 'The Red House', but there were already several other houses with this name in the city. Upon consulting the Post Office Mrs Johnson was told: "If the Dean wants his house to be called 'The Red House', he must have it. Who has a better right to the name than he!"

The Red Dean died in Canterbury October 22nd 1966.

Dame Sybil Thorndike described him as a man of 'heartening courage'. Paul Robeson had believed him to be 'loved all over the globe.' An unnamed colleague of his who had known him from his 32 years in Canterbury was less charitable when he referred to him as 'blind, stupid, deluded, unreasonable and a public nuisance.' Whatever your view, certainly a character.

Grandfather of Australian Ornithology

JOHN LATHAM (1740-1837)

A Dartford medical doctor was the first to describe, and to name scientifically, a great number of birds, many from the Antipodes, which were brought back from expeditions as skinned specimens. But as well as identifying birds from all over the world, John Latham is credited with being the first to describe two very characteristic birds for Kent - the Dartford Warbler and the Kentish Plover.

Latham was born in Eltham, Kent on June 27th 1740 where his father was a practising surgeon. Little is known of his early life but he must have been well educated as he was admitted to a London hospital to study medicine. He seems to have had a keen interest in natural history from an early age as by the time he is general practice in Dartford in his early twenties, he is corresponding with the leading ornithologists of the day: Sir John Edward Smith, Colonel Montague, Thomas Pennant, Sir William Jardine, Sir Ashton Lever, Sir Joseph Banks and many others.

For a positive identification of a new species it was necessary to get hold of a real bird, so this invariably meant shooting it. Latham had been observing Dartford warblers for some time in North Kent and describes them in his notebook: 'They feed on flies, springing from the bush on spying one within its reach, and returning to the same perch repeatedly; in this imitating much the manners of our Cinereous (Ash-coloured or Spotted) Flycatcher.' Latham had seen the bird on the heather and gorse-covered commons of Dartford and Bexley Heath, Shooters Hill, Blackheath, Keston, Hayes and Bromley but it was not until a friend had shot a pair on April 10th 1773 that they were positively identified as a new species.

The same was the case for the Kentish Plover. The surgeon of Sandwich, William Boys, obtained a dead bird and sent it to Latham who declared it a new species on May 23rd 1778.

A General Synopsis of Birds written by John Latham came out in three volumes between 1781 and 1785 and in this he used the vernacular names for the species he described. In later works he went over to the Latin names which came to be accepted as the normal practice for their classification. Because of his growing reputation almost all specimens that were brought back from expeditions to the Antipodes and the Pacific, including Captain Cook's second and third voyages, were inspected by Latham, identified and classified by him. Many of them were new to science such as the emu, white cockatoo, wedge-tailed sea eagle, lyrebird and magpie. He wrote up the descriptions of the birds in *The Voyage of Governor Phillip to Botany Bay 1789* after the return of that pioneering expedition and he knew more about the birds of Australasia at the end of the 18th century than anyone else, even though he had never been there. Which explains why later he came to be known as the 'Grandfather of Australian Ornithology.'

Latham was elected a Fellow of the Royal Society in 1774 in recognition of his scientific work and later, in 1788, became a founder member of the Linnean Society, named after the famous Swede who had died ten years earlier. Carolus Linnaeus was also a physician and naturalist and was the founder of modern scientific nomenclature for plants and animals. Nearly 3,000 of Linnaeus's books, as well as hundreds of specimens of plants, minerals, insects and manuscripts had been bought by one of Latham's scientific friends, Sir John Edward Smith, for a thousand guineas and upon his own death in 1829 the Linnean Society had bought the same important scientific collection from the executor's of Sir John for £3,150. The Swede's collection has remained in the safe keeping of the London-based Linnean Society ever since.

In 1796, Doctor Latham retired from being a general practitioner to the inhabitants of Dartford and two years later moved to Romsey in Hampshire. He continued his studies of natural history in retirement and between 1821 and 1828 he brought out ten volumes of *A General History of Birds* - he designed, etched and coloured all the 193 plates in these books himself. He was a great one for visiting museums and created one of his own - he not only stuffed and set up all the birds and animals but put together most of the cases in which they were exhibited.

His enquiring mind remained sharp right up until his death on February 4th 1837 in Winchester; he was buried in Abbey Church, Romsey. One of his acquaintances, Dr Gray wrote to another in their scientific group just after the funeral: 'I do not think my fellow naturalists have sufficiently appreciated the talent of this extraordinary man, for so I consider him, when I think of the difficulties he had to encounter and the variety of his acquirements both as a naturalist and an antiquarian, above all, the extraordinary activity and great energy of his mind at the advanced age (96) in which it was my great pleasure to become acquainted with him.'

John Latham

Dr John Latham served the people of Dartford loyally for many years, administering to their aches and pains and trying to keep them healthy in mind and body, but he also dominated ornithology for over half a century. His scientific work was acknowledged by his being elected an honorary member of the Berlin Natural History Society and of the Royal Society of Stockholm - which puts him squarely in the front rank of European scientists of his time.

 * * *

Will the real Christopher Marlowe please stand up!

CHRISTOPHER MARLOWE (1564-1593)

The night of Wednesday May 30th 1593 was hot and humid. There was an electrical storm with lightning as bright as day with echoing thunder crashes. In the top room of a Deptford inn, four men could be heard arguing. They had been there all day, continually drinking. Downstairs the landlady, widow Eleanor Bull, hovered in indecision. She welcomed their custom and wanted to make sure their glasses were kept full. At the same time, there was something menacing in the sounds of their quarrel.

The voices upstairs grew louder and suddenly there was a scream so loud and terrible that passers-by in the street heard it and hurried away on their own business.

Eleanor Bull waited no longer and came up the stairs two at a time. She was a seasoned publican and it would by no means be the first fight she had seen or helped to pacify. But on this occasion she was too late. Reaching the top of the stairs, she saw that one man lay dead on the floor. His assailant (it was learned later) had been Ingram Frizer, who had struck so hard with a knife above the right eye that the blade had penetrated the brain, causing instant death.

The murdered man was Christopher Marlowe, the great dramatist, said by some to be the originator of serious tragic drama in England. He was just 29 years old. The two other men were Nicholas Skeres and Robert Poley.

That then is the conventional account of the death of Christopher Marlowe. But over the past four centuries, historians and researchers have raised questions to which it is impossible to give certain answers.

We know that a Christopher Marlowe was born in Canterbury in 1564, the son of a local shoemaker. He was educated at the King's School in Canterbury and Cambridge University. We know also that shortly after the murder, the name of Christopher Marlowe appears in the burial records. But can we be certain that it was Marlowe? The face of the murdered man was so savagely disfigured that it was unrecognisable. Investigators had only the word of the murderer and his two companions for identification.

Elizabethan spelling is notoriously variable and unreliable. Scholars have identified a whole series of names in the records. During his Cambridge days, there was Marlin, Marlen, Marley, Marly, Marlyn, Marlye and Merling - and there are probably others still unearthed. He was also given other name variations at different stages of his life.

The man we know as Marlowe was more than a dramatist. It seems clear that he was one of a whole army of spies employed by the state. The three other men at the inn where he was murdered were also spies. But it's by no means certain that they knew this about each other.

Christopher Marlowe was a bad choice for a spy. He was volatile, argumentative and outspoken in an age when free speech was dangerous. He was also a man who had transgressed the laws of the time. On the day of the murder, there was

Christopher Marlowe

already a warrant out for his arrest. Word was given to the authorities by Thomas Kyd, a fellow playwright, with whom Marlowe had shared rooms. The rooms were ransacked and treasonable papers found. Kyd insisted they were Marlowe's.

The charges were blasphemy, treason and homosexuality. But instead of being thrown into prison, Marlowe was ordered to report to the Privy

Council daily. Typically the records show two different spellings of the name in as many days. But why was he not thrown into prison, which would have been the norm? Were his spymasters protecting him? It is interesting to note that in the papers giving Marlowe's connection with the secret service, his name is spelt as Morley.

There are other accounts of Marlowe's end. Marlowe's patron and spymaster Thomas Walsingham, may well have been embarrassed by the wayward Marlowe. Could he perhaps have ordered Marlowe's assassination? In the trial over the playwright's death, the jury found that the killer had acted in self-defence.

Marlowe's life and death are full of question marks. And over the years, many scholars and historians have put forward a number of possible alternative scenarios. Was it possible, for example, that Christopher Marlowe had nothing to do with the events of May 30th 1593? That he was not even there? He wasn't killed but simply died of the plague? Another body could have been substituted? Or - on another tack - was the murder set-up to enable Marlowe to escape trial? In this version, he wasn't killed at all - he simply slipped away.

An even stranger theory comes from Calvin Hoffman, an American critic. In this version, Marlowe goes into hiding and continues to write plays - but under the name William Shakespeare! To add credence to the argument, the American points out that Shakespeare 'disappeared' between 1584 and 1592. Critics also point out that Shakespeare's work of 1592 was not as good as Marlowe's. Perhaps Marlowe didn't want to put his name to his early works at this stage. Hoffman also cites examples of references to Marlowe's previous works in the plays of Shakespeare.

Or maybe the conventional tale is the true one after all.

Whatever his end, the facts about Marlowe's beginnings are not disputed. His first school years were probably spent in parochial classrooms. Then in January 1579, he won one of 50 scholarships to the King's School in Canterbury. Every Christmas he was granted 2 $^1/_2$ yards of cloth for his school gown and he received £1 for each of the first three quarters of 1579.

At the end of 1580, he won an Archbishop Parker scholarship to Corpus Christi College, Cambridge. The matriculation register has his surname 'Marlin', without a Christian name being stated. Marlowe (or Marlin) attained his BA in 1583 and his MA four years later. It seems likely that by this year, 1587, he had completed his first major work, *Tamburlaine*, although it was not licensed for publication until August 14th 1590. This masterpiece was written mainly in blank verse and - a dangerous thought in Elizabethan England - questioned the existence of God.

Dr Faustus, followed in 1588, *The Jew of Malta* in 1590 and *Edward II* soon after that. He wrote a number of poems and songs, his best known *Come With Me And Be My Love.* In 1592, the plague raged through London and all the theatres were closed. Marlowe used the time to write his epic poem, *Hero and Leander.* Sadly, it was never finished.

What then is the verdict on Christopher Marlowe and the many mysteries written about him? In William Urry's *Christopher Marlowe and Canterbury,* the author seems ready to accept the conventional account of Marlowe's manner of death. In fact, Urry feels that with Marlowe's disposition, the end - sooner or later - was inevitable. He writes: 'There is no need to invent a plot to put Marlowe out of the way.' Marlowe's temper came easily and Urry cites four other occasions in which the poet was involved in violent struggles with other men. But, he believes, it was just such a temperment that is part of the creative spark that produced his writing genius.

'The surges of excitement generating his mighty verse were very close to the sudden rages which convulsed him. The same passion which sustained him as a poet destroyed him as a human being.'

Child of Wonder

ARTHUR MEE (1875-1943)

Omnivorous, insatiable curiosity was the driving force behind one of the most prolific writers that there has ever been. Arthur Mee claimed to write a million words a year and if he had not died at 68, he could well have written himself into the *Guinness Book of Records*. Although born outside the county, Mee moved to Kent in 1904 and lived here for the rest of his life, drawing inspiration from the bluebells and beech woods and riverside pastures of the Darenth Valley.

Arthur was born the eldest son and second of the ten children of Henry Mee, a railway fireman, and his wife Mary Fletcher, both devout Baptists in Stapleford near Nottingham on July 21st 1875. He attended the village school and his headmaster there, George Byford, encouraged the young lad, who right from an early age displayed a zest for knowledge and an infectious capacity for wonder.

In Victorian times if you came from a working class family, the opportunities for education, particularly further education, were limited, and at 14 Arthur left school and got a job as a copy-holder in the printing works of the *Nottingham Evening Post*. His job was to read aloud from the copy (probably hand written as typewriters, or Remingtons, were only just being developed then) while the proofreader checked each word on the galley proof.

This was his daytime job. In the evenings, he would go and read to a local baker, a kindly old man called Henry Mellows, who was a fine Methodist preacher and deeply interested in current affairs. There were not enough hours in the day for the baker to do all that he wanted to do, so he invited Arthur to come to the bakery after his work to read aloud the previous day's parliamentary report. This allowed Mr Mellows to work and learn, as all the time he was kneading dough and baking bread and cakes.

At 16 years of age, Arthur was articled to the *Nottingham Daily Express* and he set about becoming a top-notch journalist, an excellent occupation for someone who was fascinated by all things and all people. Small of stature, neat of appearance, busy and alert, he taught himself shorthand which was to prove so useful when interviewing. He also developed a skill for speed writing which he honed by taking down sermons in chapel on Sunday evenings. He was so good at his reporting that at 20 he was offered, and he accepted, the job of editor on the *Express's* subsidiary, the *Nottingham Evening News.* His wage was £2 a week.

As well as editing the paper, Mee had also been contributing articles to *Tit Bits,* a magazine available nationally and owned by Sir George Newnes, who recognised a fine journalist in the making. The publisher invited Mee to become a staff writer for his stable of publications which included *The Strand Magazine, The Westminster Gazette* and *Country Life* and so the Nottinghamshire young man removed to London.

Once established in the capital, Mee continued to write prodigiously. He churned out six substantial columns a week for one or other of Newnes's publications and he edited a picture magazine as well. Within a couple of years he had also written two political biographies, a book about Edward VII and another tome titled *England's Mission by England's Statesmen.*

Arthur Mee

In 1897, Mee had married a Yorkshire girl, Amelia but usually called Amy, and they lived in Tulse Hill in London. But when their daughter Marjorie arrived, they looked for a place in Kent and moved to Uplands, a large house in Hextable. The house had five acres of grounds, with immaculate flower gardens, croquet and tennis lawns, a conservatory, a vinery and a peach house.

Mee was now working for Alfred Harmsworth (later Viscount Northcliffe) as his literary editor on the *Daily Mail.* When his boss got to hear about Mee's personal collection of 250,000 cross-indexed press cuttings, which he had built up over the years, he asked his enterprising employee to come up with ideas on how they could be utilised.

First to be published was a *Self-Educator,* a vast work spread over the years 1905 to 1907 - this established Mee as an able organiser of popular instruction and a master of both graceful phrase and forceful slogan. In 1908, he started *The Children's Encyclopaedia,* a result of his little daughter's persistent questioning and her father trying to answer them in a way that a child could understand. It was published as a part work every fortnight and was so vividly written and profusely illustrated that it was an immediate success, appealing to both children and their parents. Part of its originality was that it did not have the conventional alphabetical arrangement, but was divided into 19 groups, which came out in small manageable sections.

Group Seven was titled 'Wonder' and sub-titled: 'Plain Answers to the Questions of the Children of the World.' Even if not all the answers are wholly satisfying there is no hesitation about tackling the largest and most intractable issues. 'Why do I laugh and cry?' receives the direct answer: 'You laugh and cry because you are made that way.' But it is not left at that, for it continues: 'A very good and beautiful reason for the tears we are really making all the time we are awake is because they keep the eyes clean' and the item ends with Mee giving an insight into his character. 'Let us not shed too many tears in this beautiful world.'

When the part work was complete it was published in a single volume and the dedication on the book reads: 'Inspired by Marjorie Mee. Suggested by Amy Mee. Edited by Arthur Mee.' In the USA it came out as *The Book of Knowledge* in 1912. Because the system of article arrangement was obscure, much of the success of the work as a reference tool resulted from its splendidly contrived index, which even today remains a model of its kind.

There followed a whole string of books, many for children: *History of the World, Natural History, Popular Science, Arthur Mee's Hero Book, One Thousand Famous Things, The Book of Everlasting Things, The Children's Bible* and *The Children's Shakespeare*. When the History of the World was launched, Mee came up with the slogan '10,000 pictures from 10,000 years'. Being both honest and with a fondness for neatness and rounded numbers, he kept his pictorial staff perseveringly on the job until they had unearthed at least 9,000.

When Miss Marjorie Mee was interviewed on the 100th anniversary of her father's birth in 1975 she revealed an interesting fact about her father; his shy and retiring nature, albeit with a natural grace and a merry laugh. "He must have been fond of children," she said. "But he could not stand and talk to them. He was not good with children. He much preferred to write for them."

Mee's biographer, Sir John Hammerton, whose book is aptly titled *Child of Wonder,* picked up the same theme: "His extraordinary gift for communicating with children through the written word was because he did not adopt a schoolmaster pose but wrote in the most natural way for their complete understanding. This was because he was always a child himself and could instil even the simplest things with some essence of the wonder that possesses all young persons in their early contacts with life and the realities of nature."

In 1913, Mee was involved in launching the *Children's Newspaper* which he edited until he died in 1943. It came out weekly and ran until 1963. He considered this the most satisfying of all his achievements because it 'told the story of the world today for the men and women of tomorrow with an unconquerable faith in goodness and progress.'

Needless to say with his myriad ideas and boundless energy to carry them through to publication he made a good living. Uplands in Hextable was a large country residence that would require gardeners and housekeepers and cooks to ensure that the family enjoyed the lifestyle they had become accustomed to. His salary in the first years of the 20th century was an annual £3,000; this allowed him to buy a building plot on top of Eynsford Hill and he had built an imposing house, which cost £16,000 in 1914. In the garden, in a wooden shed overlooking the beautiful sweep of the River Darenth, he would do his writing. There below him was a Roman villa, Norman church, a ruined castle and a cluster of old cottages - quintessential Kent. Later in the grounds he built a second house, where his daughter Marjorie lived.

For the last ten years of his life, Mee, in addition to all his other writings, was working on the volumes of *The King's England*, a survey of 10,000 towns and villages. Although he was helped by a group of colleagues to travel the half a million miles he estimated the work necessitated, each of the 40 volumes bears the mark of Arthur Mee, who edited the series into a whole. He himself visited every town, village and hamlet in Kent to gather first hand information, preceded by his wife Amy who would be on the look out for interesting inscriptions on graves, and the like, for her husband to follow up. Although the books have been updated and reprinted since, they are still very much the work of the original author/editor.

Arthur Mee was a product of his times, a writer who had an enormous influence over young people. Hammerton describes his ideology as composed of Christian ethics, love of England, belief in the British Empire as an instrument of moral and social welfare and a reverence for heroes and heroic achievement. Mee retained none of his father's grim doctrinal exclusiveness, except for one thing: temperance. With this in view, he inaugurated a Strength of Britain movement, which flashed brilliantly for a time and then faded harmlessly away.

Mee's greatest gift was that he was always enthused in what he was doing, yet not for money he might make out of it nor for the influence on opinion it might give him, but for the sheer love of knowledge, no matter how arcane. At the time of his death on May 27th 1943, suddenly and unexpectedly following an operation in King's College Hospital, tributes came in from all over the world. Lord Northcliffe said of him: "Arthur Mee had a capacity for ideas that amounted to genius". At 68, much to the chagrin of his chief employer who had benefited hugely from those ideas, there were to be no more.

Dandified Spa Ruler

RICHARD 'BEAU' NASH (1674-1761)

Richard Nash, nicknamed 'Beau' because of his reputation as a dandy, put the spa town of Tunbridge Wells on the social map in Georgian times; it became, in the summer months, a place where the rich and fashionable of London came to see and be seen. Nash ruled over the town as a monarch ruled over his realm, ensuring that rules were kept and decorum maintained, as taking the waters and gambling attracted the raffish and rakish elements of society as well as the upper classes. According to historian G H Trevelyan: 'During his long supremacy as Master of Ceremonies ... Nash perhaps did as much as any person even in the 18th century to civilise the neglected manners of mankind.'

Nash was born in Swansea on October 18th 1674. His father Richard had a glass factory which was successful enough for him to be able to afford a good education for his son. From Carmarthen Grammar School he went to Jesus College, Oxford but his time there was spent in the pursuit of pleasure rather than the pursuit of academic excellence and he left without a degree. In fact, the principal of the college sent him down after he had become romantically involved with a young woman to whom he had proposed marriage. His indulgent father then bought him a commission in the Army. The young Richard rather enjoyed the dressing up and the mess dinners, but not the actual soldering. He spent money on his uniform, dressing the part 'to the very edge of his finances' but as for drilling and performing arduous duties, these were not to his liking so he sold his commission and resigned.

Next stab at a career was the law and he entered as a student of the Inner Temple in 1693. There he distinguished himself by his good manners, and led such an insouciant way of life without visible means of support that his close friends suspected him of being a highwayman. The fact was that he was a successful gambler, mostly at cards, but he would also accept wagers to carry out dares. On one occasion he rode naked through a village on the back of a cow and another time he won 50 guineas by standing at the great door of York Minster as the congregation came out, clad only in a blanket.

But his showing off did not prevent him from being serious when he needed to be. His organisational skills were first displayed in 1695 when he was selected by his fellow students of the Middle Temple to superintend the pageant which they exhibited before William III. This so impressed the monarch that he offered to make him a knight, but Nash graciously refused the honour as it did not come with any money. He knew that it was hard enough living by your wits without having to continuously keep up a life style demanded by a title.

His love of gambling drew Nash to the West Country spa of Bath. The fortunes of the place had risen after a visit by Queen Anne in 1703 who went there to take a health cure.

Richard 'Beau' Nash

When Nash arrived two years later, his organising skills were soon to be displayed. Being of an agreeable nature but with an imposing bearing, he was accepted by both visitors and the town dignitaries who realised that rules were needed for the season to be a success.

One of the first changes that Nash made was to ban the wearing of swords. Just after he had arrived in Bath, his predecessor, Captain Webster had been killed in a duel. With so many young bucks swaggering around town trying to impress the young and fashionable women, sword fights were not uncommon and honour could only be upheld by duelling. Nash thought this a completely uncivilised way of resolving real, or imagined, wrongs and if swords were not worn in public then the risk of injuries and deaths from rash hotheadedness was reduced.

A whole series of improvements followed: smoking in the company of women was banned; the sedan chair carriers, notoriously rude, were made to be more polite; a strict dress code at the balls was enforced; patrols to protect visitors from brigands and footpads were introduced; entertainment and music were provided. Even the appearance of the place was improved for Nash organised a public subscription which raised £18,000 to improve the roads in and around Bath. By such displays, Nash became the unquestioned autocrat of Bath, the veritable arbiter of all social affairs.

The success of Bath as a fashionable resort did great harm to the more sedate spa of Tunbridge Wells. But those who made a living from welcoming the rich and providing for them realised that the key to their success was the way that Beau Nash had brought order and social caché to the summer season. So the Kent town dignitaries asked the man to come and preside over their season as well, but instead of competing with Bath, they decided to extend the season so that the great man himself could officiate at both Bath and Tunbridge Wells.

Nash had visited Tunbridge Wells on a number of occasions prior to his accepting the position of Master of Ceremonies. But his arrival to take up his duties was something else. Over the years his vanity had grown and he liked to dress the part with embroidered jackets and lace cuffs and collars. He always wore an immense cream coloured beaver hat, knowing full well that its uniqueness insured against it ever being stolen. He arrived at the Pantiles in 1735 in a post chariot drawn by six high stepping greys with outriders and footmen, who made sure that no one could miss the occasion by blowing loudly on their French horns.

Nash's presence during the season in Tunbridge Wells ensured that the Kent spa prospered. Visitors came as much for the gambling and the flirting as for taking of the rust-coloured chalybeate waters. Nash himself continued to gamble and had a stake in the business as well. When gambling on the popular card games played in the spa resorts was made illegal in 1739, Nash shrewdly realised that the best way to keep the punters coming was to invent new games not covered by the law.

A resident of Tunbridge Wells by the name of Cook devised a game that Nash introduced into the Assembly Rooms. It was like roulette and called Even and Odd or EO. The table had 20 even and 20 odd numbers and the players betted against one or the other. However the ball could also fall into two long holes, besides E and O, and in that case the bank won which meant that the overall odds were very much in the house's favour. It became a favourite game for the gamblers in both Tunbridge Wells and Bath and Nash joined the inventor and the proprietor of the gambling house in a share of the profit.

Nash was very generous to anyone in need - especially with other people's money. Once an entry into the accounts of the gaming house was questioned; Nash had written: 'For making one man happy 10 shillings.' When asked to explain this he said: "I heard a poor man say to his wife and large family that 10 shillings would make him perfectly happy. I gave it to him to see if it would. It did. If you disapprove, however, I will refund it." The proprietor roared with laughter and doubled the gift. Nash was different from many who frequented the gaming rooms; a moral if vain man, he would never cheat the naïve young bucks although many others would have no scruples about doing so.

At dances he was very protective of young women warning them against adventurers, although he himself had had something of a reputation as a ladies' man.

He was a stickler for rules. If dancing was to stop at 11 pm then it did. Once the daughter of George II, Amelia, demanded another dance after that time. "Remember, I am a Princess," she added haughtily. "Yes Ma'am, but I reign here and my laws must be kept," he replied, and they were.

In the 1740s, the owners of the gambling halls at both Tunbridge Wells and Bath began to cheat Nash, who was no longer so diligent in preserving his business interests. He decided to resort to the law to claim the money owed to him, but only succeeded in showing the world that a gentleman who was insistent on good behaviour and social niceties, was himself living off the proceeds of gambling. For one so witty and clever at put downs in the gaming and assembly rooms his performance in the court was surprisingly inarticulate. Subsequent gossip began to diminish his reputation.

Investigations into EO turned into a scandal - as the odds were unfairly stacked in favour of the house. Further laws were passed affecting gambling, and gaming came to end in the spas in 1748; this was the beginning of the end for Nash as his main source of income dried up. He sold his fine clothes and moved into a smaller house which left him with a small lump sum which produced a little income which he lived off.

His friends, knowing he would accept no charity, opened a subscription list for a book that he was supposed to be writing: *The History of Bath and Tunbridge Wells for These Last Forty Years with an Apology for the Author's Life.* Orders at two guineas each were substantial and continuous and the money was passed to him which saved him from his creditors. Considering Nash had done so much for the towns of Bath and Tunbridge Wells, a monthly pension of ten guineas from the Bath authorities was somewhat measly.

In 1752 he was taken ill in Tunbridge Wells with apoplexy and his last recorded visit to the town was in 1755. He went to live in Bath where a former courtesan, Juliana Papjoy, looked after the rather sad and embittered old man. The King aka Beau Nash died in his sleep on February 12th 1761 having lived through seven reigns and into the beginning of an eighth.

Inventor of Modern Journalism

ALFRED CHARLES WILLIAM HARMSWORTH
VISCOUNT NORTHCLIFFE (1865-1922)

Lord Northcliffe - whose favourite house was Elmwood in Broadstairs, Kent - was probably journalism's first genius. He was a man of enormous power, sometimes acting as a world statesman who felt he could make or break governments and change the course of the First World War. When he died in 1922, a burnt-out case at 57, tributes poured in from all over the globe.

His own paper, *The Times,* ran some three pages about its proprietor. But even its rival, *The Daily Telegraph,* admitted that Northcliffe had had 'one of the most remarkable

Alfred, Harmsworth, Viscount Northcliffe

careers of modern times' and that 'his influence upon affairs extended far beyond the bounds of Great Britain'. From the *Pall Mall Gazette:* 'The English press has lost its most romantic and outstanding figure and public life one of its foremost personalities. Few men have had a greater influence upon the history of British newspapers or upon their methods or ideals'.

Alfred Harmsworth, the great reformer, was born at Chapelizod, near Dublin on July 15th 1865, the same year that Abraham Lincoln was assassinated. He was the eldest of 13 children. His father, also called Alfred, was an English barrister, working at the Irish bar. His mother was Irish, the daughter of a Dublin land agent. In 1867, the family was forced to flee Ireland, after threats by the revolutionary Fenians.

The young Alfred was remembered by those who knew him as being exceptionally studious, energetic and eager for knowledge. After a period when he attended dames' schools, at 11 he was sent to Stamford grammar school in 1876, and in 1878, as a day boy to Henley House, Hampstead (then kept by John Vine Milne, father of A A Milne), near his parents' new home.

It was during his first year at Henley House that Alfred made his first foray into journalism by starting a school magazine. It appeared first in manuscript form and then in print, the type set up by Alfred in his spare time. Critics later said that this early writing showed something of the freshness and vivacity that marked his later work.

However, the young Alfred was largely self-educated: when he was 15, his father's health broke down and the lad - together with his very capable mother - was left to bring up the surviving seven boys and three girls. The relationship with his mother was very close and throughout his life, hardly a day went by when he didn't visit her or a week when he didn't sleep under her roof; when he was abroad, he would write or telegraph.

Alfred's first paid writing was carried out for a friend of the family, Mr Jealous, editor of the *Hampstead and Highgate Express*. The remuneration, he remembered later, was very modest. His parents wanted him to go to Cambridge and they hired a tutor for him. Alfred however, had little inclination for a university career and spent most of his time writing freelance contributions to *Bicycling News* (he was an ardent cyclist), the *Globe,* and the boys' and girls' papers, published by a James Henderson. Alfred always remembered Henderson as his 'first journalist sponsor'.

About this time, he travelled extensively in Europe with a friend of his father's. He continued to send in freelance pieces, one on fireworks to a magazine called *Youth,* published by the *Illustrated London News.* On his return, Alfred met the proprietor of the ILN, who eventually offered him the post of assistant editor of *Youth,* at a salary of a guinea and a half (£1.60) a week.

He accepted the post, kept on with his Cambridge tutor at night, and bombarded other publications with his freelance work. His first editorship was with a short-lived educational monthly. He came into personal contact with the great men of the major dailies and wrote later that he was unimpressed with their methods of working. The budding entrepeneur was already eyeing his potential rivals in the market place.

In 1882, when he was 17, Alfred left home for rooms at 6 Pump Court, Temple. He continued to write articles for anyone who'd buy them and did much of his library research at the British Museum. He was complimented for his style but still got his share of rejections. This, he said later, did him a world of good. He read omnivorously and loved the classics.

In 1884, he took a bicycle ride from London to Bristol in pouring rain on an empty stomach. The result was a violent attack of pneumonia which made him susceptible to chills for the rest of his life. Medical advice was that he should live out of London. In 1885, he took a job in Coventry with a firm call Iliffe, among whose publications were the *Midland Daily Telegraph* and *Bicycling News*. It was the perfect position for the future Lord Northcliffe, for it gave him experience in every different department of journalism.

Through his London contacts, he had two books published - *One Thousand Ways to Earn a Living* and *All About Railways*. Before he was 21, he was offered a partnership by Mr Iliffe but - having saved about £1000 - he was determined to return to London and eventually strike out on his own.

In 1887, at the age of 26, he formed his own publishing company. In June 1888, after various other ventures, he launched *Answers to Correspondents* (later shortened to *Answers*). Alfred was joined by his second brother, the future Lord Rothermere. Some typical articles included Strange Things Found in Tunnels, What the Queen Eats and Why Jews Don't Ride Bicycles. The 1870 Education Act had spread literacy amongst the population and opened a whole new market for newspapers and periodicals.

Alfred saw to the training of new editors and artists, changing the whole system of periodical journalism with new ideas and fresh approaches. He also hired some of the greatest writers and thinkers of his generation - among them H G Wells.

He used brilliant promotional devices. His most successful, run in December 1889, promised the winner £1 a week for life if he could estimate all the gold and silver held in the Bank of England. Each entry had to have five supporting signatures who were readers of Answers - so with 700,000 entries, he gained 3,000,000 extra readers at a stroke. The business prospered and was soon yielding a profit of over £50,000 a year, a substantial sum. By 1892, overall sales rose to over 1,000,000 copies.

His next enterprise was boys' papers, with their circulation soon overtaking the competition. As A A Milne put it, 'Harmsworth killed the penny dreadful by producing a ha'penny dreadfuller'.

Now having the money to stretch his wings, Alfred made an extensive tour of Europe, America and India. He was also able to afford the first motor cars which started arriving from France and was among the earliest amateur drivers. On August 8th 1899, he was involved in the first recorded car accident in Kent (some say in England).

In August 1894, he acquired the *Evening News,* then operating at a colossal loss. But with the efforts of Alfred and his brother, the paper was to bring in a profit of £14,000 in the first year.

On April 11th 1888, Alfred had married Mary Elizabeth, daughter of Robert Milner, of Kidlington, Oxfordshire, a West India merchant. They honeymooned at 18 Alexandra Gardens, Folkestone, went to live in an old house in Hampstead, and spent their summers in Broadstairs, Kent. They initially boarded there at Flint Cottage, Nelson Place, and at 36 Albion Street.

They came upon Elmwood by chance. In his memoirs, friend and author Max Pemberton, tells the story. 'Returning from an expedition to Sandwich one day, we drove through the village of St Peter's and beyond it the ancient village of Reading Street ... At a turning of the village street, our ancient horse decided upon a little self-reflection and, pausing to admire the view, he allowed us to see over a high wall beyond which lay as beautiful a garden as Thanet could show'. They found that it was for sale and purchased it - despite the fact that someone else was convinced he had already bought it!

Alfred and Mary moved into Elmwood in April 1891, after Liberty's of London had carried out the furnishings and decoration. The house proved to be incurably damp but the family loved it. First a billiards room was added then extensive stables - which eventually garaged Northcliffe's growing fleet of cars. In 1898, he bought the adjoining Joss Farm.

Alfred loved the sand and the rocks but didn't care much for sea bathing. However, he believed in the beneficial effects of sea water and left instructions that his morning bath be filled with sea water and heated. Then one day he discovered that the gardeners had been filling his bath with water from the pond, adding a piece of seaweed or two for authenticity!

Other houses followed. There was Sutton Place, a splendid Tudor mansion in Surrey. And in London, 1 Carlton Gardens, 36 Berkeley Square and 22 St James's Place. But Elmwood in Kent always remained the family's favourite.

In the general election of 1895, Alfred stood unsuccessfully as the Conservative candidate for Portsmouth. It was not his only failure. According to the *Dictionary of National Biography,* whenever he emerged from his world of newspapers and attempted to play a part in public affairs, these times 'were the least conspicuously successful of his life'.

On May 4th 1896, he founded the *Daily Mail.* Sold at a halfpenny, it promised the most news in the least space. Northcliffe ran a remarkably efficient news service, a full system of cables and the best writers he could buy. During the Boer War, sales were over 600,000 copies a day. He achieved another journalistic first, by introducing duplicate printing - carried out in London and Manchester.

In 1903, he founded the *Daily Mirror* as a paper for women. When this didn't work, he converted it into a halfpenny illustrated daily - another first. In 1905, he was raised to the peerage as Baron Northcliffe. In the following year, he decided to invest in the raw materials of his papers. He and his brother, Lord Rothermere, acquired 3,000 square miles of forest land in Newfoundland and established the second largest paper mill in the world.

One particular Northcliffe dream was realised in 1908 when he bought *The Times,* in the face of several others competing for the purchase. For some time, he kept in the background, making changes slowly, reluctant to interfere too quickly with the paper's proud traditions. He even kept the existing chairman in his place. He consulted with the editors and left them free to carry out the policies agreed upon. At the same time, he had the latest printing machinery installed at Printing House Square, appointed new correspondents all over the world, improved cable services and strengthened the staff in all departments. Working hours were shortened and salaries increased. The reward was a successful newspaper with increased circulation.

As a public figure, Northcliffe warned against increasing German armaments and advised the admiralty to maintain a strong Navy.

Among Northcliffe's wide interests was aviation and in 1906, he arranged a *Daily Mail* prize for the first flight between London and Manchester. This was won in 1910 and it was repeated a second time. He then offered a third £10,000 prize for a flight across the Atlantic; this was won in 1919 by the British airmen Alcock and Brown in a British Vickers-Vimmy biplane.

In his first speech in the House of Lords, Northcliffe advocated a build up of British aircraft on a large scale. He took a similar interest in submarines and made two descents, one hazardous. He also strongly recommended the introduction of compulsory military service and ran a campaign to persuade others to his way of thinking. Obtaining the necessary support in parliament, a general call-up went out in 1916.

During the First World War, the *National Review* described him as 'the great driving force in our country'. He was not afraid of being unpopular and in 1915, criticised Lord Kitchener for the shortage of ammunition and the lack of high explosive shells. This provoked an uproar. Copies of his papers were publicly burned, he was excluded from many public institutions, advertisements were withdrawn and paper sales fell.

'Better lose circulation than lose the British Empire', was his response. He was nevertheless proved right and won great popularity for his actions. In another public move, he was instrumental in obtaining an evacuation of the stricken armies in Gallipoli. It was also pressure from Northcliffe that brought down the failed Asquith government and made Lloyd George prime minister. Northcliffe pressed for a vigorous campaign against the German U-boats and - in the face of abuse - insisted on the need for food rationing.

A further proof of Northcliffe's influence was the reaction of Germany. The Germans published the *Anti-Northcliffe Mail* and struck an anti-Northcliffe medal. In February 1917, his house in Broadstairs became the target of a German destroyer's gunfire. Shrapnel crashed through the roof and smashed the library windows; Northcliffe slept through it all. Sadly, not everyone remained unhurt. A shell crashed through the south wall of the gardener's cottage, killing Mrs Morgan, the gardener's wife, and two of her daughters, Phyllis and Doris.

Northcliffe paid a number of visits to the various front lines and sent back war dispatches to his papers. Lady Northcliffe maintained a private hospital of her own in which she worked as a nurse.

Lloyd George offered Northcliffe various jobs in the government, all of which he declined. He was then asked to go to America as chairman of the British War Mission to the United States. Once there, he co-ordinated various British missions which were then spending some £10,000,000 a week. He maintained close relations with President Wilson and the government and went on a number of tours across the country, gaining good will for the British cause. On Northcliffe's return to England in November 1917, the king promoted him to the rank of viscount.

In February 1918 he agreed to become Director of Propaganda in Enemy Countries - a position he carried out with outstanding success. German generals complained that their troops were 'literally drenched with enemy publications' and that Northcliffe was 'that most thoroughpaced rascal of the Entente.'

However, the war years took their toll. Never one to enjoy robust health, Northcliffe began to suffer from hoarseness in the throat. In 1919, he underwent an operation when an adenoma was removed. His great disappointment about this time was not getting an invitation to the Peace Conference.

On May 1st 1921, he spoke at a luncheon for the 7,000 members of his staff on the *Daily Mail.*

Northcliffe then embarked on a world tour, during which he spoke out bluntly to his hosts, advising the Australians of the potential 'Asiatic peril,' which might be the outcome of their 'white Australia policy'. He admonished the Japanese for their militarist ambitions in China and declared that the Anglo Japanese Alliance had outlived its usefulness. He pointed out the grave consequences of Gandhi's propaganda in India and warned of the repercussions of Muslim unrest in all the countries of the Near and Middle East. Throughout the tour, he continued to send back dispatches to his newspapers.

But Northcliffe's world tour was his last great effort. He reached Marseilles in February 1922 a sick man. Despite this, he appeared at several functions in his honour in London and made a private visit to Germany (where he was convinced that his enemies had poisoned him).

He died on August 14th 1922, shortly before his 57th birthday, at his London home, 1 Carlton Gardens, of infective endocarditis. He was honoured with a funeral service in Westminster Abbey - which had recently been the beneficiary of a large restoration fund from *The Times.* Lord Northcliffe was buried at Finchley.

Darent Valley - Close to the Magical Workings of God

SAMUEL PALMER (1805-1881)

The Darent Valley was the inspiration for a 19th century painter who founded an artist's colony in Shoreham - he referred to it as his 'Valley of Vision'. Though only 20 miles from London, the landscape setting that so inspired Samuel Palmer is almost as unspoilt and stimulating today as it was when the artist lived here between 1826 and 1833. It deserves to be included in the Kent Downs Area of Outstanding Natural Beauty.

Samuel Palmer was born on January 27th 1805, the son of a London bookseller. A delicate and highly sensitive child, he was educated at home for several years by his father who taught him Latin and Greek and encouraged a love for the Bible and English literature, especially the classical poets like Virgil, Milton and Bunyon. When he was 12 his mother died and the young lad was distraught but the nurse that he had had since the age of three, Mary Ward, was still working for the family and she comforted him. In fact Mary, the surrogate mother, stayed with him until she died in 1837.

After a short spell at the Merchant Tailors' School, Palmer received private tuition to become a painter and at 15 had three landscapes accepted by the Royal Academy. He began to meet other artists, including John Linnell, his future father-in-law. But the painter who had the most influence over him was William Blake, whom he first met in 1824. Although Blake was 67, and had but three more years to live, his imagination and powers of design were at their highest at this time.

Never in robust health, father and son decided to leave London, described by Samuel as 'the great national dust hole', and they came to Kent, with ever-faithful Mary Ward to be housekeeper. They settled in Shoreham as much for the fresh air as the feeling that Samuel had that here, in the Darent Valley, he was close to the magical workings of God. The 21 year old was a zealous believer and in this quiet Kentish village surrounded by hop gardens and orchards, with water meadows and woods, the spiritual images of the Old Testament and the classical poets seemed to take on the reality of literal truth. He looked a bit like a prophet himself - he wore his hair long, had a flowing beard and wrapped himself in an ankle length cloak.

Having been left £3,000 by his grandfather, Samuel used the inheritance to derive a small income. At first the family rented a little cottage, dubbed 'Rat Alley' for obvious reasons. But then they moved into the Water House, a Queen Anne dwelling on the banks of the Darent. Friends came down to join them and an artistic colony developed. Edward Calvert was one of the first to arrive and declared that Shoreham 'looked as if the Devil had not yet found it out'. Then followed Francis Oliver Finch and George Richmond - all of them aspiring artists - and they were joined by kindred spirits with romantic temperaments, like stockbroker John Giles and Frederick Tatham, a man of private means. They dubbed themselves 'The Ancients' as they looked back to the halcyon days typified by pastoral idylls and spiritual simplicity.

They were a cheerful, intense brotherhood all deeply into unorthodox religion who lived frugally on tea and bread and butter. They would go for long walks around Shoreham by day and night, talking boisterously. Often they would still be out at daybreak to see the dawn, which would inspire them to paint later in the day. And in the evenings they could chose from Palmer Senior's library of books that he had thoughtfully brought with him.

At Underriver near Sevenoaks painted by Samuel Palmer

Other artists visited to enjoy their Spartan hospitality and stimulating talk of mysticism and meaning. Blake came down for a visit not long before he died. The great artist was a clairvoyant. Sitting at the kitchen table, he declared that Palmer was coming up the road from the village. The others present told Blake that Palmer had gone up to London by coach that morning. Just then the door opened and in walked the young artist - the coach had broken down and the trip had been cancelled. On another occasion, Palmer and Calvert had gone with Blake to look for a ghost in Shoreham Church.

Many of Palmer's works during this time were directly inspired by and named after actual places in the vicinity: *Rooks Hill, At Underriver near Sevenoaks, The Hop Garden, The Weald of Kent.* He went on to become a sought after artist with his paintings changing hands for hundreds of thousands of pounds. He was considered notable enough for the great forger Tom Keating to copy his works and the Mellon Collection in the USA has some of his paintings, as does the British Royal family. Most critics believe that Samuel Palmer's painting style, reaching its peak during his time in Shoreham, was years ahead of his time and an important inspiration for Graham Sutherland and John Piper a hundred years later.

But the colony disbanded in 1833, helped no doubt by the intrusion of reality into a rural idyll. The riots prompted by the repeal of the Corn Laws touched the Darent Valley and several ricks were burnt. Palmer moved back to London and he fell in love with John Linnell's daughter, Hannah. When his housekeeper, Mary Ward, died in 1837, he married Hannah and they set off for a two year grand tour of Europe. They returned to spend the summer of 1840 with his wife's parents in Underriver where he did some more painting of Kent scenes.

Further visits to Kent followed over the years, staying with the in-laws. But the family home was in London. Unfortunately two of their three children died in infancy and Palmer's creativity was affected by this. He still managed to do some work, mostly etchings and water colours but his latter years were darkened by doubts and disappointments.

But he did not forget Shoreham, and what it had meant to him as a young man - the mist coming off the River Darent, the venerable oaks in Lullingstone Park, the sheep grazing in the orchards on the walk along the river to Otford. Long after he left Kent, he wrote about 'the raving mad splendour of orange twilight on landscape ... I saw that at Shoreham.'

He died at Furze Hill House, Mead Vale, Redhill on May 24th 1881.

✳ ✳ ✳

Lifelong Hunter Collector

MAJOR PERCY HORACE GORDON POWELL-COTTON (1866-1940)

Percy Powell-Cotton was the founder of one of the most eclectic museums that is to be seen in the country, let alone the county. Quex House near Birchington on the Isle of Thanet had been in his family for five generations and the museum began in one room of the house in 1896. Today there are eight galleries and the museum, a charitable trust, is still growing but the great majority of the exhibits were obtained by Percy who, between 1887 and 1939, went on 28 collecting expeditions, mostly to the Indian subcontinent and Africa. He devoted his life to the collection and study of fauna and ethnography.

John Powell, who worked for the Crown and was a close colleague of the paymaster general to George III's forces, had bought the original but then derelict Quex House and the estate that went with it, in 1774. The finance for this was somewhat dubious and Powell may have been involved in a money laundering operation with the connivance of his

Major Percy Powell-Cotton with pygmies

boss. The 14th century house was rebuilt between 1805 and 1814 as a Regency building and succeeding generations of the family created an estate that was virtually self-contained with a brew house, bake house, laundry, larders and store rooms, workshops, stables, coach house and servants quarters. Percy's great grandfather built The Sea Tower in 1814 as a lookout and signalling station and in 1818 The Waterloo Tower to celebrate the victory over Napoleon. This tower houses a peal of 12 bells which were offered to the local church but the vicar declined the gift; it is one of the few secular peals in England and is still in use, being rung regularly by the Quex Society of Change Ringers.

By the time Percy inherited the property in 1894, the family had married into the Cotton family who had had close connections with the East India Company (his great-grandfather had captained an Indiaman and spent most of his life at sea). One of the rooms is known as the Oriental Room and the furniture is Indian and Chinese, acquired by his ancestors from trading trips to the Far East.

Percy's upbringing was conventional enough, coming from a well off family. He was tutored privately and then a captain's commission was bought for him in the militia in Northumberland; he subsequently rose to the rank of major but there is no evidence that he actually served in the regular Army nor did he see active service.

Percy's first overseas trip was to the North East Provinces of India in 1887 but his next three were proper collecting expeditions to Balistan, Kashmir and Ladak. These expeditions were partly funded by like-minded sportsmen and gentleman collectors as well as bankers like the Rothschilds, and the British Museum. With such funding he could afford to go away for months at a time. For his expedition to Uganda and the Belgian Congo in 1904 he was away for three years (he went on to spend 26 years of his life on African soil). While in Africa at this time he married Hannah in Nairobi; she was 25 years his junior and had been his secretary. She seems to have shared his passion for collecting and going to remote and dangerous places as they honeymooned in the Cameroons. Hannah's personal collection of African butterflies and other insects can be seen at Quex.

As for Percy, his main interest was animals, and collecting in those days meant shooting and skinning and having the subjects stuffed, usually by the London taxidermy company of Rowland Hall. He corresponded extensively with his taxidermist, detailing exactly what he wanted him to do. The museum has 894 letters that passed between them. Over the years, he amassed 6,000 skins and 4,500 skeletons of different birds and animals including such rare specimens as the flightless scaly tailed squirrel. Paradoxically, his collecting by killing animals was because he was worried about animals losing their natural habitats and becoming extinct. Fortunately the skins were dried (not tanned) using arsenic in the bush and field, and this allowed them to be preserved indefinitely.

On the 1904-06 expedition, Percy came close to being killed ... by a lion. A wounded animal had taken cover in thick bush and dry elephant grass. The hunting party moved cautiously towards where they thought the animal was hiding, throwing sticks and clods of earth to try and flush it. Suddenly it charged and the white hunter, usually such a good shot, fired both barrels but failed to stop the beast in its tracks. Percy reached out instinctively for his second gun but the rifle bearer had fled. As he turned, the lion leapt on his back and knocked him to the ground and began raking him with his claws.

Two braver natives ran up and using a stick and a whip tried to get the animal to let the hunter go; they distracted the lion long enough for a Nubian guard to shoot it dead at close range. Upon inspection it was found that the lion had a broken jaw and this saved Powell-Cotton for if the animal had been able to clamp his jaws on the hunter he would surely have been killed. As it was he had 17 claw marks on his back but he had been saved from further serious mauling by a copy of *Punch* in his back pocket. The clothing worn by Percy at the time of the attack as well as the stuffed animal itself is on display at Quex along with his .400 double barrel and his Mannlicher rifles. This was Powell-Cotton's 13th lion and it was shot on a Friday.

Powell-Cotton's expeditions may have had another motive as well. He had unprecedented access to remote areas, like Abyssinia, and upon his return to Britain, he would report to the Foreign Office - a spy whose cover was scientific research? When photography came to be more common, Powell-Cotton shot more animals on film than with a gun. The collection has 25,000 images and 70 moving pictures going back to 1927.

The collection of animals at Quex is shown in dioramas, which were something of an innovation over 100 years ago, before the invention of colour photography. Although rather dated today, they still give a dramatic representation of the animals in their natural setting with trees and grass and painted backdrops; one was painted by a Belgian soldier patient as a gesture of gratitude as the house had been taken over as a Voluntary Aid Detachment (Red Cross) in the First World War. One of the exhibits had to have its case specially constructed, including the floor lowered - it is thought to be the biggest elephant to have come out of

Africa with Rowland Ward charging £250 to prepare it for showing to the public. Also on display are what are thought to be the heaviest pair of tusks taken from an elephant shot by a European. They weigh 198 lbs and 174 lbs respectively.

In addition to the specimens on public display, the museum possesses fine study series of skins, skulls and skeletons, the value of which is enhanced by careful and detailed notes made by the naturalist in the field. In particular, the collection of 400 specimens of gorilla and chimpanzee is unequalled in the world and is extensively consulted by scientists. Some of these beasts were obtained from another hunter/collector, Fred Merfield, who was getting skins and skeletons from the native African hunters who killed the animals for their meat and had no use for the skins and skeletons. Such avid collecting of monkey-like creatures was a product of the age, as there was huge interest in Darwin's belief that man was not created but a result of evolution.

Unusual forest and swamp animals to be seen at the museum include the bongo, the sitatunga and the giant forest hog. One diorama, representing a jungle scene in the Central Provinces of India by moonlight, is dominated by a prowling tiger but also includes a leopard up a tree, which has just seized a four-horned antelope; in the background are two sloth bears. There is also a nilgai or blue bull which was the first large specimen shot by Major Powell-Cotton. The tiger skin in this Indian case was in store for over 40 years before being mounted, which is a tribute to the initial preparation after skinning and the great skill of the taxidermists who worked for Rowland Ward.

The ethnographical collections are interspersed with the animals and are particularly important because many of the tribes have either died out or been assimilated since Powell-Cotton observed them a 100 years ago. The Didinga exhibits are of interest, for the only occasion when the Major's caravan was ever attacked was by this tribe in 1902. After some porters' loads had been stolen on the march, his camp was under siege for three nights with the natives preventing him and his men from getting any fresh water. Two of his men were killed and the porters' morale was flagging, but the man who had enlisted voluntarily in Northumberland's citizen army led his men through the enemy territory and eventually reached the Nile, without further loss.

Some 30 years later in the same area, the Major gave a lift to a man with a scarred face. By coincidence, he was a chief who had been involved in the attack and with a grin he pointed to his face and said, "Yes, I remember, you gave me that." He bore no malice and seated on a tree trunk, surrounded by the elders of the tribe, the two former adversaries reminisced about the incident.

The Powell-Cottons had four children and they sometimes accompanied their father on his expeditions. The eldest daughter Diana (1908-1986) went on the Somalia expedition of 1934-35 and made a collection of the stock owners' crafts including wooden stools and pillows, spoons and combs, personal ornaments, knives, grindstones, milk and butter pots. The Somali travelled widely and for generations were in contact with Arab culture which is reflected in the comparatively advanced artefacts on display of surgical instruments and even a wooden door lock.

As well as craft items, Powell-Cotton collected textiles, musical instruments and weaponry including swords, arms and armour from Burma, China and Japan. There is also a collection of Japanese netsuke, Pacific Island ethnographic artefacts, archaeological items from local diggings on the Isle of Thanet carried out by another daughter Antoinette (known as Tony), Napoleon Bonaparte memorabilia and the Major's personal collection of travel and sporting books including the two that he wrote *A Sporting Trip Through Abyssinia* in 1902 (he was appalled by the numbers of elephants that gentlemen hunters were killing, often using the animals as target practice) and *Into Unknown Africa* in 1904.

Percy's son Christopher is still going strong (84 at the time of writing) and lives at Quex and takes a keen interest, as chairman of the governors, in the museum founded by his adventurous father. Back in the 19th and early 20th century, expeditions were hazardous undertakings into unknown and sometimes hostile territories. The Major wanted to preserve rare and representative specimens and was more a naturalist than a big white hunter. He, no doubt, would have approved of the motto of the museum: 'In Trust for the Enjoyment of Visitors and the Benefit of Students.'

Percy died in 1940 and is buried in a private mausoleum on the estate.

Influential in the Abolition of Slavery

REVEREND JAMES RAMSAY (1733-1789)

A vicar of the Kent village of Teston played a significant part in the movement which eventually led to the abolition of slavery. The Reverend James Ramsay is buried in the churchyard of his own church and he lies alongside an African by the name of Nestor, whom he had rescued from a life of slavery when he was 14. For the next 22 years Nestor had been the vicar's servant until his death in 1787. The important difference, of course, is that servants worked for their masters, while slaves were owned by them.

Little is known of Ramsay's early life after his birth in 1733 but he clearly came from a family wealthy enough to afford to give him an education which allowed him to enter the Royal Navy as a surgeon. In those days the life on board ship was harsh and the job of sailing one of His Majesty's vessels throughout the expanding world could be quite dangerous. The rigging of ships consisted of blocks and tackle and huge areas of canvas which had to be set or furled by the sailors as the ship pitched and bucked and heaved, especially in bad weather.

Surgeons were needed not just in the time of war when they had to operate in primitive conditions below deck - amputating shattered limbs or setting broken bones - but their skills were needed when accidents occurred. Any member of the ship's crew could be thrown about, especially in a storm, and Ramsay himself suffered a bad fall while on deck and this brought to an end his career at sea.

His ship at the time was stationed in the West Indies and Ramsay sought a position on the island of St Kitts. The small and mountainous volcanic island had been discovered by Columbus in 1493 and named after his own patron saint of Christopher. It was the British settlers who arrived in 1623 who shorted the name of the island to St Kitts and it was these settlers who successfully established Britain's first colony in the Caribbean. By the time Ramsay came ashore in the middle of the 18th century, the island had been divided into parishes and successful sugar plantations established on the rich volcanic soil.

Ramsay was ordained and became a rector of two parishes on the island which, although was in the path of the trade winds and could be hit by hurricanes, usually enjoyed a healthy climate. It must have been a pleasant life, not too warm because of the sea breezes, but with lanes and farms and churches just like back home in England. But the vicar was troubled not so much by the way of life of the colonists, which was suitably pious and church-going, but by the appalling conditions of the Negro slaves who had been brought from Africa to work the sugar plantations. An estimated quarter of all those brought across the Atlantic by ship at this time died on board (and were thrown over the side) while of the remainder, a further 30% to 50% were dead after three years in the West Indies.

The rector's great aim was to convert the slaves on St Kitts to Christianity and to improve their living conditions because, at worst, they were treated like animals. Needless to say his work for his black parishioners brought him into direct conflict with his white ones. They

Reverend James Ramsey

accused Ramsay of disrupting the work of their plantations by making the slaves say their prayers and the white slave owners walked out of church when he prayed for the Negroes' conversion. Feelings ran high on both sides but what Ramsay saw and heard then stayed with him for the rest of his life - and it was this experience that convinced him that slavery was morally wrong.

In 1781 Ramsay became vicar of Teston, on the Medway above Maidstone, and immediately found himself in a society of Evangelicals and philanthropists. Sir Charles Middleton, later to become First Lord of the Admiralty, lived in the parish at Barham Court and Ramsay was not only his vicar but also his good friend. Ramsay was a frequent visitor at the house and would meet, dine and wine and discourse with other like minded individuals including Doctor Johnson, Hannah More (dubbed 'the bishop in petticoats') and William Wilberforce who had become an MP in 1780.

Ramsay not only argued amongst the intelligentsia about the evils of slavery he also wrote a treatise which played an important part in making the case for the trade's abolition. His *Essay on the Treatment and Conversion of African slaves in the British Sugar Colonies* came out in 1783 and the MP for Hull, William Wilberforce, read the essay eagerly. By this time Sir Charles Middleton had been elected an MP also, for Rochester, and his wife was so shocked by Ramsay's descriptions of conditions in the West Indies that she urged her husband to raise the subject in parliament. To do this he needed allies and the young Wilberforce was to be one of these; he was invited to visit Teston and meet Ramsay to hear, at first hand, what the slave trade was like. Following this meeting Wilberforce determined to make the abolition of slavery his life's work.

Ramsay was a powerful ally in this task and a prominent member in the early pressure group which campaigned for abolition. He wrote several important pamphlets on the subject, one of which was presented to each member of both houses of parliament. But his old enemies, the plantation owners, rose up to attack him again and fought back with treatises and pamphlets of their own. They were not averse to using dirty tricks - they sent Ramsay several parcels of stones on which he had to pay the postage. A fierce assault was launched on Ramsay's character and he was not above replying to the planters in the same low forms of abuse that they employed on him.

The vicar became increasingly annoyed by these personal attacks and they could well have affected his health. He died suddenly in 1789, the same year that Wilberforce had first proposed the abolition of the slave trade in parliament (it was to be nearly another two decades before the trade was actually abolished in the British Empire in 1807). But the good vicar had played his part and should be remembered for his courage and fortitude in speaking out against the vested interests who could see no wrong in the inhuman trade.

The memorial to him on the east side of the church at Teston is a bit florid but in typical 18th century fashion is a fitting tribute to a Kent character we should be proud of: 'While firm Integrity, Unaffected zeal for the Public Good, Steady contempt of Self interest, Tender attention to each Social duty, Benevolence to the Whole Human Race, And Humble Piety to God Are held in estimation: The Memory of the Revd. JAMES RAMSAY (Whose earthly Reliques are here deposited) Will claim respect, Mingled with sorrow, that his Labours Were no longer spared To the Poor, the Friendless, and the Oppressed, For each of whom of whatever Clime or Colour His Christian Love, & generous exertions Not disappointment could exhaust, Calumny slacken, Or Persecution abate.'

Jewish Family of Distinction

THREE GENERATIONS OF SALOMONS

Broomhill, an impressive country house between Southborough and Tunbridge Wells, was the home of three men from three different generations who were all called David Salomons. Between them they lived there from the end of the reign of George IV to the middle of the reign of George V, in all just short of a hundred years. Each David was a remarkable character in his own right.

The first David was born in 1797 and died in 1873. It was he who bought Broomhill in 1829; back then it consisted of an estate and a small villa in the Italian style which the sales document describes as a 'genteel residence' with tree reception rooms, five bedrooms and a water closet, a very 'modern' installation. Although only in his early thirties, David had already made his mark, and was beginning to add to the family fortune, from stock-broking and merchant banking in the City of London (he was one of the founders of the London and Westminster Bank). But like many City types then and now, he wanted a place in the country for weekends and for holidays.

As well as his business activities, the first David was very active in public life and it was by his efforts in this field that he is best remembered; not only was he wealthy and hard-working and ambitious, but he was Jewish. By testing the law and insisting on change, Salomons made it possible for people who could not take an oath of loyalty 'on the true faith of a Christian' (because they weren't) to hold positions in public life. It may seem difficult to believe today but

Sir David Salomons

back in the 19th century, Jews, Unitarians and members of some Christian sects like Quakers were almost completely excluded from public life, as also from a naval or military career, from the civil service and even from academia. It was not until 1870, for example, that anyone who was not a member of the Church of England could be an undergraduate or professor at Oxford or Cambridge Universities.

David Lionel Salomons

In 1830 the Common Council of the City decided that the oath of allegiance need not be a Christian one but one held to be binding to the individual person, according to his religion. This change allowed Salomons to become a liveryman of the Coopers Company in 1831 (a privilege later granted to the other two Davids). In 1835 he saw the opportunity to take the next step in opening up public life to Jews and he entered the election for the office of Sheriff of the City. He was successful but the oath (again a Christian one) stood in the way to actually assuming office but the government stepped in and passed a law abolishing this oath.

In 1838 he became the first Jewish magistrate in Kent and a year later further honours followed - he was appointed by Queen Victoria to the position of High Sheriff of Kent. The next barrier to fall was to become the first Jewish Alderman of the City in 1847 and in 1855 he reached the culmination of his municipal career - he was elected Lord Mayor of London. During his term of office, one particular act bears witness to his life long struggle for religious toleration. Up to 1855 the Monument, commemorating the Fire of London in 1666, had an inscription which ascribed the fire to the malice and hatred of the Roman Catholics. At his insistence this was removed.

Prior to this, David Salomons had recorded another first. He had fought a number of elections to try and get elected to parliament and not succeeded - Shoreham 1837, Maidstone 1841, Greenwich 1847 - but in a by-election as a liberal, again in Greenwich in 1851, he was elected. He declined to take the oath 'on the true faith of a Christian,' but nevertheless insisted on voting three times without having been sworn in the statutory way. Prolonged legal proceedings followed and he was fined £500 (even the judges knew the law was a nonsense and could have fined him £500 for each vote but decided on a 'token' fine). Eventually in 1858 the parliamentary oath was changed and became binding on the conscience of the member not his Christian religion.

For the rest of his life David Salomons represented Greenwich as their MP. In 1869 he was created a baronet with special dispensation that it should pass to his nephew upon his death, as he had no children neither by his first wife Jeanette nor by his second Cecilia. In fact he had largely brought up his nephew, David Lionel, and his two nieces at Broomhill as his brother Philip and his sister-in-law Emma had both died young.

The second David, who inherited Broomhill in 1873, had completely different interests from his uncle. He took a small part in public affairs, although he did not evade such offices as naturally came his way as a local landowner and man of wealth. In particular, he made many benefactions (including the Royal Victoria Hall in Southborough) and served as Mayor of Tunbridge Wells from 1894-5. Like his uncle, he was a JP, a member of the Kent County Council and also filled the offices of High Sheriff and deputy Lieutenant of the County. But the second David is best remembered for his fascination with science and machinery, and his inventions.

The first David had had a house in London as well as Broomhill, but it was the second David that gave the Kent estate his full attention and transformed the buildings on the property to what you see today. The first addition was the water tower, completed in 1876, and new waterworks which he designed. On top of the tower he installed a telescope for his astronomical studies. Four years later he had completed the huge wing of workshops and theatre forming the northern half of the house. It took 100 local men from Southborough and Tunbridge Wells two years to complete the work and David acted as the architect, engineer, surveyor and site contractor throughout. The bricks were made from clay dug locally and the sandstone was also from the estate's own quarry.

The workshops were the best equipped in private hands anywhere in the country and he used the laboratories to develop his pioneering work in electricity. He installed electric light in Broomhill, having in many cases to invent the appliances, meters, lamps and switches. He was a great one for gadgets and made an electric butter churn, an electric sewing machine and an electric iron - forerunners of the household appliances that were to become commonplace much later. He was also interested in photography and in various matters of medicine, especially in the use of X-rays, equipment of which he not only presented to a number of hospitals but installed it as well.

His theatre was used for all sorts of special effects - colour photographic backdrops, the sound of thunder and phonographic reproductions of the human voice. He ordered an organ from the Welte company of Freiburg in Germany and this remarkable instrument, the largest of its kind in the world and consisting of many thousands of valves and pipes, was worked entirely by electricity. It cost £4,050 and arrived in Kent just one week before war was

David Reginald Salomons

declared in 1914. It was assembled in the theatre by Steinway & Sons. Unfortunately silent since the death of Sir David, it awaits restoration.

Apart from the appliance of science to electricity and photography and even early experiments with telephones and wireless messages, his other great passion was promoting the horseless carriage. He organised the first motor show in England at Tunbridge Wells in 1895 on the agricultural showground off the Eridge Road (now the Showfields Estate). There were five vehicles on display - the total number of horseless carriages in Britain at that time. There was his own Peugeot, the Panhard-Levassor of Evelyn Ellis (the only other privately owned car), a motorcycle, a fire engine and a steam engine towing a carriage. It was not illegal for them to be driven on the public highway but it was illegal for them to exceed 2 mph, as they were discriminated against by the

Locomotives Act of 1865. The same restrictions did not apply to horse transport, or even to cyclists, so motorists were harassed not for driving, but for speeding.

Because of these restrictions, Sir David got up early and transported the vehicles from Broomhill to the show field. He returned to Broomhill to collect his family and guests in a horse carriage to see the vehicles. When he arrived back on site he unhitched the horses and posted a notice HORSELESS CARRIAGE, which was his idea of a joke.

As his interest in motorcars grew, Sir David adapted the splendid stables at Broomhill and they remain what is probably the finest example of early motor-carriage housing anywhere in Britain thanks to his customary expertise in all aspects of design and building and his eye for detail. These five garages (still with their original floors and hinges) had cavity walls, central heating, tongued and grooved boarded ceilings, inspection pits (at just the right depth for chauffeur/mechanics to stand in) and a spiral staircase leading down from the chauffeur's quarters (formerly the groom's) above.

In 1896 Sir David founded the Self-Propelled Traffic Association and became its first president. This was the forerunner of the Royal Automobile Club. He also worked tirelessly to get new laws for motorists and is said to have written no less than 65,000 letters in his campaign for the motorist to be able to use the public highways albeit at no more than 14 mph. When the act was finally passed in 1896, it fell to him to draw up all the necessary technical clauses because no one else in the country knew sufficient about the subject.

At the New Year David Lionel used to send his friends small booklets of aphorisms and other *bon mots* that had occurred to him during the previous twelve months. 'Never pat a strange dog with no tail to wag' and 'collecting is a form of madness, but a graceful insanity when applied to works of art.'

With a son and heir, David Reginald born in 1885, and two daughters, the second David of Broomhill must have been contented with his life of invention and scientific experimentation. But tragedy was to strike.

The third David had had a privileged up-bringing thanks to his wealthy family. After Eton he had studied at Gonville and Caius at Cambridge, and following university, he had travelled extensively in the Far East and on returning to Britain he had busied himself with working for the Territorial Army. With the approach of war, David Reginald had raised a detachment of men from round and about where he lived in West

Kent; many were the sons of neighbours in Southborough and High Brooms. After the outbreak of war, these men became part of the 1/3 Kent Field Company, Royal Engineers and David Reginald was given the rank of Captain.

He and his men were sent out to Gallipoli in 1915 and on October 28th their troopship, the *Hythe,* was laying off shore under blackout conditions waiting to land. Another ship the *Sarnia,* under heavy Turkish fire, began to pull away from the shore after disembarking its troops and it collided with the *Hythe,* slicing off her bow. It sank in ten minutes. Captain Salomons refused to leave, standing on the bridge and encouraging his men to keep cool and save themselves. He even gave his lifebelt to one of them, and when he was urged to save himself his last words were: "No, I will see my men safe first." The memorial to Captain Salomons and 128 men of the company who also drowned is in St Matthew's Church, High Brooms, about two miles from the family home of Broomhill (now called Salomons). Sir David Lionel Salomons lived a further ten years and with his death in 1925, the baronetcy ceased to exist.

Success Not on the Beaten Path

SIR MARCUS SAMUEL (1853-1927)

Shells gathered on the beach at Margate lead to the naming of one of the first truly global companies that is still going strong today, being active in 140 countries and with 140,000 employees worldwide. Back in the early years of the 19th century, the Kent coastal resort was a popular choice for Londoners who wanted sea breezes for themselves and sand for their children to play on when they took a holiday. The Samuel family was hard working and Jewish and lived in the East End and they took their summer holidays at Margate. One year the children noticed shells on the beach and they collected them and stuck them on the box that had contained their lunch. They were so pleased with their handiwork that they brought it home and showed it to their parents. It gave their father an idea ...

The result was that shell-covered Victorian objet d'art - jewellery boxes, bowls, antiques, curios, bric-à-brac, photo and picture frames, pincushions and blotters - became a speciality of the Samuels and were sold in The Shell Shop in Houndsditch. The business did so well that the family imported shells from the Far East and then employed about 50 people to arrange them and stick them on the bare wood.

Marcus Samuel was the son of the founder of the family shell business and when he took it over in 1878, he began travelling abroad to buy the curios and shells that were needed to continue and expand the business. Other lines were added to the company and general produce and rice was also imported. Like many an entrepreneur before and since, Marcus kept his eyes

Marcus Samuel

and mind open to new ventures. On one business trip to the Black Sea in 1890, his attention was drawn to oil tankers in the harbour at Constantinople that were supplying kerosene oil to markets in the Orient.

He quickly grasped the concept of bulk transport but it wasn't until he had come up with a way for the ship to carry freight in both directions that the economics began to make sense. Up until then it was considered impossible to clean an oil freight carrier for a return journey with another commodity like rice. But Samuel overcame this by cleaning out the hull with steam, a practice suggested to him by a captain in the merchant marine service.

A fleet of eight tankers was ordered and the first, the 5,010 ton *Murex*, made her maiden voyage through the Suez Canal in 1892 with 4,000 tons of Russian kerosene from Batum bound for Singapore and Bangkok. The tankers for this new venture had been designed by Sir Fortesque Flannery to satisfy the stringent need of the canal authority. Samuel then began setting up bulk storage for oil in Far East ports and assisted by financial support from other members of the Anglo-Jewish community, most notably the Rothschilds, within five years he was in a position to suggest a consortium of companies that would work together in trading with the Far East. This company was named the Shell Transport and Trading Company, in honour of the original nature of the family business.

For a time the British company encountered a serious rival in the Dutch Petroleum Company which obtained its oil from Java and Borneo - being that much nearer to the markets of the Far East, the Dutch company could undercut the freight charges of Shell, which was transporting its oil from Russia via the Black Sea and Suez. In consequence Shell turned its attention to Borneo and set up business there. The success of this move caused the Dutch company to prefer partnership to competitive trading, and in 1907 the Royal Dutch Shell Company was formed, making it a single large oil producing, refining and distributing organization.

Samuel had been knighted in 1898 for services rendered in the salvage of HMS *Victorious*. In February of that year the naval ship had run aground off Port Said and she had been pulled clear by two of Shell's tugs. With the coming of war, Shell again offered its services to the nation. Every form of petroleum was made available wherever it was required either for the land or sea forces. Also a petroleum distillate, which formed the basis of the high explosive TNT (trinitrotoluene) was provided in large quantities. A refinery was established near Bristol for this purpose, the construction of the works being carried out in a matter of only weeks, thanks to the energy and insistence of the company's boss, Sir Marcus Samuel.

In 1901 oil was discovered in Texas and Samuel arranged with one of the producers to transport and distribute it internationally. That made Shell Transport the first oil company with worldwide sources of production for supplies of kereosene, gasoline and fuel oil.

As well as a success in his business life, Samuel was also prominent in public life, particularly in the City. Another member of the Anglo-Jewish community and Kent resident, Sir David Salomons, had done much pioneering work in breaking down prejudice and barriers to public service for Jews, and Sir Marcus followed. In 1891 he was elected an alderman; in1894 chosen as sheriff and was Lord Mayor of London in 1902-1903. In this capacity he presided over the committee which formulated the scheme for the Port of London Authority. As in all his activities, his term of office as Lord Mayor was characterised by energy and zest for life - he paid a state visit to Brussels and other places home and abroad, as well as entertaining the French president in considerable style in the Guildhall. When his year in office came to an end he was created a baronet, and later in 1921 he was raised to the peerage as Baron Bearsted of Maidstone and in 1925 this was raised to viscount. Other honours included receiving the freedom of Sheffield and Maidstone and honorary degrees from Cambridge and Sheffield Universities.

Samuel chose Bearsted in Kent as part of his title for he had bought a home in the county in 1895 - the Mote, just on the outskirts of Maidstone, part of which was in the parish of Bearsted. It was a grand park of over 500 acres, containing deer and noted for its magnificent beeches and oaks. Its large lake was stocked with coarse fish (he and Lady Samuels liked to go fishing) and the whole estate was surrounded by a high wall. Formerly the property of Lord Romney, Samuel brought the house and all its contents and moved in with his wife Fanny (whom he had married in 1881) and their four children - Walter, Nellie, Gerald and Ida.

Victorian society was not noted for being particularly pro-Semitic, nor for being unusually welcoming to self-made businessmen from the East End of London, but Marcus and Fanny became celebrated for their kindness and generosity and made many friends in Kent. The new owner of the Mote threw himself into being a country gentleman. He never became an expert shot but he very much enjoyed his days shooting pheasants and partridges; he also took up hunting, but appears never quite to have got to grips with all the terminology involved with riding and horses. One story is told of him hunting with the West Kent

Foxhounds. He was riding a particularly spirited mount that had a double bridle with which to try and control the animal - a snaffle and curb bits. As they rode off down the road the Master of the hunt noticed that Sir Marcus was riding his horse on the snaffle only and suggested: "If I were you Sir Marcus, I would ride that horse on the curb." "Thank you", he replied "but he's trouble enough in the road."

The Mote became the centre of the Samuels's domestic world and they entertained friends and colleagues from the business world and from public life there. Lady Samuel, though shy and reserved and said never to have recovered from the death of their youngest son Gerald in action in Gallipoli in the First World War, was a charming hostess. She made her mark on the Mote with her rows of orchid houses, and a fine collection of bonsai, the miniature trees brought back from Japan by Shell tankers. Sir Marcus was a short, stout man with a very soft voice, who loved adolescent jokes; however he could not abide swearing. He was a non-smoker but liked to drink, although only in moderation. He was a strict timekeeper with an excellent memory for names and faces.

His biographer Robert Henriques, who married one of Samuel's grand daughters, tells a revealing story about him. While walking in the garden of the Mote one day it occurred to him that far more vegetables were being grown than could possibly be consumed by his household. From this he concluded that the gardeners were selling his produce for their own profit. The wages for a gardener at that time was 17 shillings a week plus a tied cottage so Samuel concluded his gardeners had to sell vegetable in order to subsist. The estate manager was told to work out a typical budget and his findings showed that a gardener with five children could not live on less than £1 a week. Samuel at once put up the wages to 25 shillings a week - but said that anyone caught selling his vegetables would in future be prosecuted. His neighbours on the surrounding estates accused him of 'spoiling the market.'

In 1908 there was much unemployment in Maidstone and he agreed with the borough that, to find work, his cricket ground at the Mote should be levelled. Sir Marcus offered to pay £1,000 towards the cost provided the borough find another £500, the balance over and above to be raised by public subscription. Work for the unemployed was also found by building a private pavilion for the Mote's residents and guests to watch the game. The ground is today a Kent county ground and the house is owned by the Leonard Cheshire Foundation and is used as a day care centre.

Asked once for the secret of his success, Samuel told a reporter: "If you want to succeed you must work with heart, mind and brain. Your ambition must be to work when you are young, not to enjoy yourself. But chiefly you want new ideas. Success is not on the beaten path."

Marcus Samuel, first Viscount Bearsted of Maidstone, died in 1927 within 24 hours of his beloved wife Fanny. They were buried side by side in the Jewish Cemetery in Willesden. At the funeral the vicar of Willington, Maidstone took as his text: 'Know ye that there is a prince and a great man fallen this day in Israel.'

✳   ✳   ✳

Dedicated to the Service of God

SAINT SEXBURGA (620? - 699)

A saint with the wonderful name of Sexburga just has to be included in a book about Kent characters, especially as for 24 years she was queen of the county as well. Not only that, there is a church dedicated to her (along with St Mary) in Minster on the Isle of Sheppey, where she founded a monastery.

Sexburga lived her life in the 7th century, a period often referred to as the Dark Ages. The Romans had given up on their most northern and western province sometime around AD 400, and Angles, Saxons and Jutes, as well as Frankish and Frisian tribes, had at first raided the country and then settled in it. Out of this hotchpotch of ethnic groups from the Continent, the English grew.

The invaders completely rejected the previous Roman civilisation - towns became ruined, trade declined and warriors established small kingdoms with themselves as 'kings', ruling by force of arms and fighting with their neighbours to settle disputes. But out of this anarchy came a kind of unity and kinship and an Anglo-Saxon set of laws written in English (not Latin) and the first to be influenced by Christianity. This was a result of St Augustine coming to England in AD 597 - the Pope in Rome had drawn the short straw for him and told him to go and convert the heathen in Britain. Imagine his trepidation as he set sail across the Channel into the virtual unknown. But he was lucky, as he landed in Kent where he was made welcome by the local king Aethelbert (or Ethelbert), whose queen, Bertha, was Frankish and had already converted to Christianity, so making the saint's job much easier. Sexburga was related by marriage to Aethelbert - she was the daughter of Anna (or Annas or Ennis), the king of the East Anglians, also a Christian, and she had married Ercombert, the king of Kent, and grandson of Aethelbert in about 640.

So Sexburga comes from several generations of Christians and it is not surprising that she was made a saint. According to the Venerable Bede, the first person to write down history since the departure of the Romans, rather than to pass it on by word of mouth, Sexburga's family was pious and holy and her father 'a very good and religious man'. Another monk, writing later in the 8th century described Sexburga as 'temporate in pursuit of pleasure, humble as a royal person, unassuming and dedicated to the service of God and her grace of form was as conspicuous as that of her mind.'

Sexburga married King Ercombert of Kent in AD 640. It would have been a kind of arranged marriage, between two royal houses. If there were ties of blood in marriages between kingdoms then there was less chance of blood being spilled to resolve disputes. After the king died in AD 664, Sexburga reigned as regent for four years before her eldest son, Egbert, became king. In turn, he was succeeded by his brother Hlothere, or Lothaire, when he died in AD 673.

After stepping down as queen regent, Sexburga asked her son for land to build a religious community, and this was given to her in Schepeye, which is the Anglo-Saxon word for Sheppey and literally means 'sheep island'. Sheep were the backbone of the economy at that time; not only did they supply wool and meat, but they were also milked and so butter and cheese could be made. Writing about a hundred years later, an account of the building of the nunnery quotes stories handed down from grandfathers to fathers to sons that 'men of old said that the sound of creaking cart and complaining harrow never stopped for thirty years,' meaning it took a long time to build, if not thirty years exactly.

The site she chose for the nunnery was on top of the hill at Minster, which was a fortified lookout post for the island commanding views over the Thames, the Swale and the Medway. Sexburga became the abbess and she admitted 77 nuns, all of whom were supposed to have royal or noble connections and were either widowed or spinsters. It was quite common for widows to become nuns at this time - if they did not wish to re-marry, and many didn't, having lived through one arranged marriage, a nunnery was the only alternative, a place where they were safe and secure and could devote themselves to prayer and good works.

Some unmarried women chose to become nuns, others were perhaps not good marriage prospects for one reason or another, or perhaps were rebellious and would not accept the husband chosen for them. No family wanted unmarried daughters hanging around at home, so if no suitable match could be made they were packed off to a convent, which in fact carried a certain amount of prestige. Whilst in the convent they could devote their life to prayer. In those days it was thought that the more you prayed for the repose of a soul, the more likely it was that the benefactor of the intercession would get to heaven.

The community had a chapel, a refectory, cloisters, kitchens, dormitory, hospital, a separate house for the chaplains, and possibly a rest house for pilgrims and wayfarers. In addition there was a farm, for this was a minster that had to be self-supporting, so there were farm buildings, land, stock and fishing rights. All the buildings, apart from the chapel, would have been built in timber and wattle and daub; archaeological evidence of the flat and hard floors from these huts has been discovered. The chapel was more substantial and made of Kentish rag stone and flint, and part of this original nuns' chapel can be seen in the present church in Minster.

The nuns were of the Benedictine order, one of the stricter ones. The day was divided into periods for prayers, devotions, and church services, duty and work. The nuns were duty bound to aid the sick, help the destitute, offer hospitality to travellers, and pray for the souls of the sick, the dying and dead. At the same time they were not supposed to leave the nunnery, mix with strangers, or become too worldly. Lay sisters and servants were responsible for the duties in the kitchen and the rest house.

The community had its own seal, which had the image of Sexburga on a

Saint Sexburga

lead weight which was pressed into the hot wax. When work was carried out in Canterbury Cathedral in the St Andrew's Chapel in 1868, several charters and documents were found. One charter had the seal of Sexburga on it and pertained to the exchange of houses in Canterbury for marshland in Sheppey, an arrangement carried out between the Cathedral and the abbey in Minster.

The good abbess did not stay long in the abbey that she had founded. She was the recipient of visions and one assumes they were carried to her by angels from God. One was very worrying - that before many years a heathen people would conquer the nation. (Later in AD 832, Danish Vikings did indeed arrive to sack the abbey and force the nuns to flee, putting some of them to the sword, and the pirates came again in AD 893). A second vision was more prosaic - that she should leave Minster and join her sister Ethdreda at another monastery in Ely. This Sexburga did and she succeeded her sister as abbess there in AD 679. But the abbey at Minster had been kept in the family as her daughter Erminhild, upon the death of her husband Walfere, king of Mercia in AD 675, went there to become the second abbess.

Sexburga died in AD 699 and was buried in Ely next to her sister. She was canonised later and her feast day is July 6th.

Hermit who Lived in a Tree

SAINT SIMEON (1165 - 1265)

Simon Stock of the Carmelite order founded a number of houses for monks to live in and serve the community, in university towns and other places in England, Ireland and Spain. Although he died in Bordeaux, France, and was buried there, part of his remains (namely his skull) was brought back to Kent in 1950 and placed in Aylesford Priory, his old home. Sometimes referred to as The Friars, the monastery had been dissolved by order of Henry VIII in 1538 but in 1949 the Carmelite order bought it back again and returned it to being a working monastery.

Little is known of Simon's early life but he is said to have been born in or near Aylesford to noble parents in the year 1165, which would make him a 100 years old at the time of his death because he died a century later. But holy men destined to be saints, by leading simple and austere lives and with much prayer, maybe could achieve such longevity even in the Middle Ages.

His life of service to God began at the age of 12 when he decided to become a hermit. He chose a large hollow tree in which to live - the trunk or stock was, in effect, his hermitage and Simon 'Stock' lived there for 20 years. Nobody knows where this tree was but it is reasonable to suppose that it was somewhere in or around Aylesford.

Hermits were part of medieval life in Kent and acted as moderators between the ruling lords and the feudal peasants. A hermit was expected to protect a serf from his lord's wrath and to settle quarrels between knights of the same class. As Simon was from noble stock himself he could talk in a way that the upper classes could understand. Frequently, hermits were educated and having been on pilgrimages to foreign lands there was an aura of religious knowledge and calm about them. Some of the hermits may have been knights, and would have known about martial arts and the treatment of wounds, and so people would come to them for treatment. Hermits were skilled in leech craft and could use the aquatic bloodsucking worms medicinally. By tradition the hermit owed no allegiance to an ecclesiastical superior. He could speak his mind and often did when people came to him for practical or spiritual help. Traditionally hunted animals could also find sanctuary with a hermit, which accounts for a number of pictures of monks comforting deer.

Hermits exercised an enormous influence on public opinion at this time. Ordinary folk admired their austerity and believed that if they could endure so many hardships living in a cell 12 feet square (the regulation size for a hermit's home) then they must have genuine contact with God. As a measure of their charisma, Peter the Hermit, a French soldier turned monk, had raised an army of 20,000 peasants and led it to Asia Minor in the First Crusade of 1096.

There is some conjecture as to why Simon chose a tree for his hermitage - of course in the Southeast there are not so many crags, islands or caves for holy men to live in, away from the public gaze. But living in a hollow tree would certainly isolate a hermit to some extent from his fellow men, especially if it was deep inside a thick Wealden forest. Then again Simon may have chosen a tree because it was still associated with pagan fertility worship and the holy man wanted to Christianise it.

Some time around 1201, Simon is thought to have given up the life of a hermit and joined the Carmelite order, which had been founded nearly half a century before by former pilgrims and crusaders who set up a community on Mt Carmel in Palestine. He then studied theology at Oxford and by 1215 had become Vicar General of the Western Carmelites. A visit to Palestine followed, and he was present at a general meeting of the Carmelites in 1237, when it was decided to pull the order out of the Holy Land and confine its activities to Europe. This was a direct result of the failure of the crusades.

English crusaders were among the first to offer them assistance and one, Sir Richard de Grey, gave them land in his manor at Aylesford on the banks of the River Medway. The first group of Carmelites settled here in 1242. The church was dedicated in 1247 and this same year saw the first meeting outside Palestine of the Carmelites who came from all over the known world at that time to elect a new Prior General, and it was the local man, Simon Stock, who became their leader. Early on, the Carmelites realised they had to adapt to the different circumstances in Europe and the General Chapter of the Order in 1247 set about doing just this. The Chapter effectively changed the lifestyle of the Carmelites from hermits to mendicants (those living solely on alms), but still with a preaching role. However their contemplative origins were not forgotten and formed a strong part in their tradition.

It was about this time that Simon is supposed to have had a vision of the Blessed Virgin in which she promised that whoever died wearing the brown scapular (two pieces of cloth hanging down the front and back and joined across the shoulders) of the Carmelite order would be saved for eternal life. This proved quite contentious but it did not stop some prominent people donning the garment on their deathbeds, just in case. Edward II and Henry I both put on the scapular, just before they died.

Although not formerly canonised, Simon was credited with two miracles (the prerequisite for gaining sainthood). On one occasion he turned some water into wine and on the other he brought back to life a cooked fish. Simon became St Simeon in 1564 when his feast day, May 16th, was approved by the Holy See for the Carmelite Order.

Today the small group of friars at Aylesford still go out into the community to work in prisons, schools or local radio. Their life of personal and public prayer and their activities serving the people of Kent is in the same spirit as their medieval forebears, and, no doubt, their local saint is very proud of them.

Our Lady of Mount Carmel blessing the scapular of Saint Simeon Stock

✳   ✳   ✳

Canterbury's Great Tycoon Benefactor

JAMES SIMMONS (1741-1807)

James Simmons made a fortune in printing and publishing and selling patent medicines and spent some of it on bringing the medieval city of Canterbury into the Georgian age by financing civic works. If his money provided paved streets and fine open spaces to stroll in, his methods may have appalled conservationists as in doing so, much of architectural and historical interest was pulled down and thrown away. But back in the 18th century there was little concern for heritage; if a building had served its purpose and was showing its age, it was easier to pull it down and start again. Back then, modernisation was, by definition, an improvement.

James was born to Mary and William Simmons on January 21st 1741. His father was a Freeman of Canterbury and a barber and wig maker. The family was comfortably off and James went to the Kings School as a scholar in 1750, leaving in 1756 to become apprenticed to Thomas Greenhill of London, who was a printer and stationer. Upon completion of his apprenticeship he became a Freeman of the City of London in 1764 and he worked there for two and a half years. But his native city was too much of an attraction and he returned to Canterbury in 1767 and was able to claim the freemanship of the Kent city by reason of the fact that his father had been a Freeman when he had been born 26 years ago. As a Freeman he was free to do business in the city.

With his apprenticeship successfully completed and the experience of applying his trade in London, Simmons' first project was to set up a quality newspaper for Canterbury and East Kent. As told in Frank Panton's biography, *Canterbury's Great Tycoon,* the established stationers and printers in Canterbury did not relish the competition which Simmons represented and they did their best to frustrate his plans. Simmons tried to set up in partnership with George Kirkby, who was taking over the *Kentish Post* or *Canterbury Newsletter,* the first Kentish newspaper, from James Abree, its founder. Opposition from Kirby's friends persuaded him at first to refuse Simmons' offer of partnership, so Simmons went ahead and started his own newspaper, *The Kentish Gazette* on May 26th 1768. By the end of July 1768, under pressure and blandishments from Simmons, Kirkby had changed his mind, and the *Gazette* and the *Post Newsletter* were amalgamated as *The Kentish Gazette* under the joint direction of Kirkby and Simmons.

But this wasn't the end of it. The Canterbury printers, Flackton and Smith, put pressure on Kirkby, who was not in the best of health, to replace Simmons in the partnership. If he refused they would set up a rival paper. They then tried to intimidate Simmons, the interloper, into agreeing not to print the paper just to concentrate on selling it from his stationery business. Simmons accused the rivals of trying to 'prevent him from obtaining a livelihood in a city where he was free born by a trade to which he has a right by legal servitude.'

James Simmons

These bold words stiffened the resolve of Kirkby; Flackton and Smith declared they would go ahead with their plan to publish a rival so a paper war ensued. *The Kentish Weekly* Post went head to head with *The Kentish Gazette,* albeit that the latter came out twice a week. Simmons seems to have relished the battle and confidently told his adversaries "nothing but experience can convince some people of their error."

Simmons and Kirkby's paper was a broadsheet of four sides, each with four columns, in easily readable print, which sold for 2 pence at first and rising to 6 pence by 1800. The title page was mainly occupied with advertisements of local significance, business arrangements and local sales. Each issue included dispatches on the wars and affairs in the American and other colonies and on the Continent; an account of parliamentary proceedings; a London newsletter, giving court and society news; and a Canterbury column which collected short news items from the city and East Kent. Editorials were non-existent. Simmons conveyed his views from time to time by way of open letters to his readers.

With a twice-weekly platform to communicate from, Simmons used this to develop other business opportunities. In each issue of the *Gazette,* there was anything up to a page of advertisements for medicines and household preparations, all of which were available from Simmons and Kirkby's own shop at the King's Arms Printing House. The two businessmen acted as agents for the manufacturers. On offer were such items as Mr Hill's Pectoral Balsam of Honey, Essence of Water Dock, Tincture of Spleenwort at 3/- a bottle or Duffy's Elixir, which was promoted as a Sovereign Remedy for Many Ills. Other items were more mundane - for example Helfts Famous Powder 'for taking ink spots out of table linens, etc, without the least injury'.

Another money-spinner was a lending library; subscriptions to which were 14/- a year or 4/- a quarter and in 1782 this was advertised as consisting of 3,545 books. A distribution service was available too - the paper could be delivered to addresses as far away as Tonbridge and, at no extra cost, the carrier would deliver the patent medicines or a library book too. In essence, it was an 18th century mail order business.

Simmons was a canny businessman and capable of hard bargaining. He printed the first edition of *Hasted's History and Topographical Survey of the County of Kent* 1778-98 in four folio volumes. The author complained that the printer wanted a £1,000 up front before a single copy had been sold, in other words Simmons had taken no financial risk at all. As well as books, Simmons would print diaries and seasonal almanacs so ensuring regular business year after year.

If his business life was going well, so too was his civic one. He was sufficiently well established to be elected to the City's Common Council in 1769 and in 1772 he served as Sheriff for a year. In 1774 he was elected an alderman for Riding Gate Ward, which lead to him being mayor two years later.

On January 11th 1776 he married Charlotte Mantell of Tenterden, a spinster 11 years his junior. There is some mystery concerning his wife as when he died, a very rich man, there were no legitimate children but there were a number of bequests and after these were paid the bulk of his estate went to his 'natural son James Simmons' - this suggests that he had a son (and a daughter, who was left £50 per year) by another woman and these children changed their surname to his. Indeed a codicil to his will left £2,000 and a house and its contents to 'my friend Ann Matton who has long resided in my family'. Most likely she was the mother of his children.

In 1787 Simmons began his work of transforming the look of the city.

The Canterbury Pavement Commissioners' job was to modernise the streets and, as the treasurer to the Commissioners, it was Simmons who was the prime mover and mainstay of this group. By the end of 1789, the Commissioners had achieved their prime objectives, and the main streets inside the city walls were straightened and new paved. Houses and buildings that had stood for centuries were sacrificed, but the people at the time considered the transformation from medieval to Georgian to be nothing short of miraculous. Hasted wrote: 'the houses throughout Canterbury were altered to a cheerful and more modern appearance; and most of the shops were fitted up in a handsome style, in imitation of those in London...'

Like many a newspaper owner since, Simmons was not averse to using the clout of his publication to influence public opinion. Towards the end of 1781, the columns of *The Kentish Post* reflected the widespread criticism of Lord North and his government. The momentum for change built up, encouraged by the local paper and in due course North's Tories were ousted and Rockingham's Whigs came into government. Simmons' contribution was recognised by the new government appointing him Distributor of Stamps in East Kent. Stamp duties were liable on all manner of transactions such as birth and death certificates; on the means of money exchange and credit; on insurance policies, wills and the like and on the selling and buying of certain goods like perfumes and hats. The duty went to the government and the distributors charged a fixed percentage for their services so bringing a useful annual income to the alderman's coffers.

Further prestige and wealth was created when Simmons founded the Canterbury Bank in 1788 in partnership with Henry Gipps and later with his uncle George Gipps, apothecary, surgeon and hop dealer of Harbledown and MP for Canterbury from 1780 to his death in 1800. The bank continued under various names until 1918 when it was merged with Lloyds Bank Ltd, who have a branch to this day on the site of the original Canterbury Bank, on the corner of St Margaret's Street and the High Street.

A story of this time, perhaps apocryphal, illustrates how influential Simmons was in the city of his birth. A customer was standing outside the bank with Simmons and Jesse White, the surveyor of the Cathedral. Simmons, looking towards Christ Church Gate remarked: "If those damned turrets of the Cathedral Gate were taken away we should see the Church Clock from the bank door. Can't you pull them down, Jesse?" "It shall be done," replied Jesse, and it was done.

On retiring from his second term as mayor in September 1789, Simmons was made a Justice of the Peace and continued to take an interest in his myriad businesses. New ones included building the Abbott's Mill in the city which produced corn flour, the St Radigund's bath house for people of either sex 'to enjoy cold bathing in privacy and convenience' and, philanthropically, he had built a number of houses for the 'industrious poor' in Wincheap.

But his biggest civic project came in 1790 when he obtained a short lease on Dane John (the largest tract of open land within the city walls) for a peppercorn rent on the understanding that he would level it (except for the existing mound) and lay out gardens for £450. When he had finished several years later he had spent £1,500 and transformed the ragged piece of pastureland into what a contemporary account described as 'an exceedingly pleasant and greatly frequented promenade for the inhabitants.' As ever, Simmons basked in the adulation of his peers and modestly remarked that 'to deserve well of my fellow citizens is the chief pride of my life.'

However, he was greatly miffed in 1795, when the authorities summoned him before the council of the Guardians of the Poor for failing to pay a Poor Rate of £8 a year due on the Dane John land for which he still held the lease. He resigned the lease in indignation and complained that he had been taken 'like a pauper to the Court of Guardians'. 'Gracious Heavens,' he wrote, 'what a return is this!' It was not the money (which in fact he paid in full) which hurt him so, but the personal affront in being summoned before the justices. 'Having expended more than £1,500, I say to you and the public at large, you are heartily welcome (to it).'

But the greatest project to tax his mind and to receive his funds over the last 20 years of his life, never actually came to fruition. Simmons had a survey conducted and it seemed the project was to go ahead but the Napoleonic Wars intervened. So the canal to link Canterbury with the sea, either at Reculver or at Sandwich was put on hold.

Simmons' election to Parliament (unopposed) in October 1806 would have given him an opportunity to resurrect the canal project, especially as Napoleon's navy had been defeated the year earlier and the threat of invasion had diminished. But an ear infection early in 1807 put an end to both the great benefactor and the canal project. Simmons had been complaining for some time about the pain on the left side of his head. A physician was called and bleakly diagnosed him to 'be in a dying state'. He died soon afterwards. The post mortem revealed a large abscess in his head, which had been discharging for some time through his left ear. He was buried in the vault in the churchyard of St Mildred's Canterbury on January 30th.

As mentioned, the bulk of his estate was left to his son James Simmons, who was most probably the offspring of his live-in 'friend' Ann Matton. When the young James reached 25 in 1815, he inherited assets and cash amounting to more than £30,000 - a vast sum in those days, which made him an instant 'millionaire'.

Father of the Steam Locomotive Engine

RICHARD TREVITHICK (1771-1833)

Some would argue that Richard Trevithick was the greatest inventive genius that Britain has ever produced. There is certainly no arguing that he demonstrated that a steam locomotive could pull laden carriages years before George Stephenson did something similar with his *Rocket*. The inventor, born in Cornwall, lead an extraordinarily adventurous life, making and losing a number of fortunes in South America - so why isn't he better known and why did he end up buried in a unmarked pauper's grave in Dartford?

Richard Trevithick was born on April 13th 1771 at Illogan in the west of Cornwall. His father, also called Richard, was a personal friend of Charles Wesley who would often visit the family when his preaching brought him to Cornwall. Not surprisingly, the elder Richard was a fervent Methodist as well as being a mine manager and engineer of great ability. Shortly after his mother, Anne, had given birth the family moved to a thatched cottage at Penpounds, near Cambourne, in the heart of the Cornish mining industry.

He went to a local school and his leaving report did not suggest greatness of any sort. 'A disobedient, slow, obstinate and spoiled boy, frequently absent and very inattentive.' But he was very quick when it came to mental arithmetic, if a little unorthodox. His maths teacher admonished him on one occasion by saying:"Your sum may be right, but it is not done by the rule". To which the precocious child retorted:"I'll do six sums to your one!"

If his mental ability made him stand out so did his physical presence. He stood six feet two inches and he was incredibly strong. On one occasion he hoisted another six-foot colleague over his shoulder and held him upside down so that he could put his footprints on the ceiling. Another little trick was for him to write his name on a beam six feet above the floor with a 56 lbs weight suspended from his thumb. Needless to say his Herculean strength and considerable height resulted in him being dubbed the 'Cornish Giant', which he put to great effect, becoming a champion wrestler in the South West.

Surrounded by machinery at home and learning from his father at work, the young man applied himself to the solving of engineering problems in the lead and silver mines locally. Flooding was the bane of the mine owners and he helped keep water out of the shafts and galleries by effecting an improvement to the plunger pump. But it was in high-pressure steam locomotion that his real genius came to the fore. In 1797 (the year he married Jane, the daughter of a foundry owner), or 1798, he made a model steam engine which ran around his kitchen table. The next step was to build a steam carriage that would run on the roads and he spent hours in a blacksmith's shop, cutting and shaping and engineering the iron to make this first locomotive. On Christmas Eve 1801 the engine was ready. With eight men aboard, in pouring rain, the steam engine puffed up the steep gradient of Beacon Hill in Cambourne. Nicknamed 'the Puffing Devil' and 'Captain Dick's Puffer' it conveyed for a short experimental trip the first load of passengers ever moved by the force of steam.

Following this initial success, Trevithick set about building a second engine which was shipped to London and fitted to a carriage in which ten people could ride. Trials were made in Tottenham Court Road and Euston Square, where the public were amazed by the sight of the fire-breathing monster tearing along the highway at 12 miles an hour! The inventor charged a shilling a ride and was doing a roaring trade until the engine got out of control and ripped up 16 feet of iron railings and ended up in somebody's front garden. This incident concentrated the inventor's mind ... why not run the engine on a specially prepared track?

Richard Trevithick

In 1804 he was ready to demonstrate his latest idea. He bet a sporting iron master in South Wales that his steam engine could haul coal and passengers along an iron track. A tram way existed between Penydaren and Abercynan, just under ten miles. The carriage was loaded with ten tons of coal and the steam engine began to puff into life - the journey was completed in four hours, which included time spent lopping trees and removing rocks from the track. This event took place ten years before the construction of Stephenson's first locomotive, and 23 years before the *Rocket* made its historic journey.

In 1807 Trevithick took charge of a scheme for building a tunnel under the Thames. The work was full of difficulties and dangers as water broke through on several occasions, imperilling the lives of the engineer and his workers. The scheme had to be abandoned just before reaching the north bank of the river, when a final wall gave way and flooded the tunnel so quickly that the men feared for their lives. Trevithick was the last to get out, having ensured that none of his men were left behind.

The next scheme that his ever-inventive mind came up with was for making iron buoys, masts and storage tanks for drinking water in ships. At the same time he appears to have suggested that vessels themselves might be constructed out of iron plates. Trevithick was requested to appear before the Navy Board to put his case. His assertion, however, that iron could 'swim' was received with derisive laughter. At this the affronted inventor turned upon the Navy bigwigs and, declaring them a 'lot of old women', stormed out of the room.

His next idea for iron tanks was for using them to supply buoyancy for raising wrecks. The experiment was tried on a sunken ship at Margate, and the vessel was successfully floated. Trevithick thought that he had proved his point but a dispute arose over the payment. The inventor told the salvagers that they take his price or leave it. When they demurred, Trevithick at once gave orders to cast loose the tanks and within minutes the ship was back on the seabed.

Around this time Trevithick succumbed to typhus fever which could be fatal. It didn't kill him but it meant that he couldn't work. He was not noted for his business skills and had no savings, and so during this period of inactivity he became bankrupt and was forced to take refuge in a debtor's prison. Relations on his wife's side came to his rescue and they bailed him out. Returning to Cornwall from London by a small trading vessel, the ship was attacked and narrowly escaped capture by a French man-of-war.

His health recovered, and there was no shortage of work for him to do in and around the Cornish mines. Always restless and ever thinking of new ways to do things, he turned to agricultural mechanisation. He invented and constructed a steam threshing machine, an engine which, after long service in the principality eventually found its way to the Science Museum in London.

The next dramatic turn in his life came about completely by chance. Peru was a big producer of silver from mines high up in the Andes and some 160 miles from the capital of Lima. However, production had fallen off considerably, mainly because the mine owners could not prevent the mines from flooding. An agent was despatched to England to arrange a meeting with James Watt and to see if a steam pump was the answer. The meeting ended in failure but nosing around the streets of London the agent came across a shop with one of Trevithick's models of a high-pressure engine. The agent took it back to Peru and tested it at altitude - at 14,000 feet it worked fine.

The following year the agent was sailing again for Britain tasked with tracking down the inventor to discuss the likelihood of him being able to sort out the problem in the mines. On the ship, quite by chance, was a Mr Teague - Trevithick's mother's maiden name was Teague and it turned out that this person was the inventor's cousin. On docking in Falmouth, the introductions were soon made, and orders placed for all manner of mining machinery and equipment.

In 1816 Trevithick sailed for Peru and arriving in Lima he found himself a national hero. He was created a marquis and grandee of Spain, and proposals were made to caste a life-size statue of him in silver. Within a short time all of the equipment from Britain was installed, up and running but when all seemed set fair the War of Independence broke out. Here was a Cornishman in a foreign country, far from home, penniless with the native people fighting amongst themselves. Trevithick thought that he had to make the most of the situation and became a soldier of fortune, fighting on Bolivar's side - but he continued inventing, this time a new type of carbine rifle, most useful in time of war.

His next adventure was to work for the Chilean government - to raise a sunken vessel laden with copper and tin using his tried and tested tanks method. For this he received payment of £2,500 - a fortune in those days. He duly invested this money in a pearl fishing operation in Panama, and lost the lot.

In the spirit of 'nothing ventured, nothing gained' he set out with a Scotsman named Gerard for Costa Rica and stayed in that country for the next four years, prospecting for gold and silver. They discovered the minerals in sufficient quantities to be mined but they needed capital to begin operations, so the intrepid pair made their way overland from Lake Nicaragua to the sea, the first Europeans to attempt such a thing. It was a hellish journey through hostile jungle and they lived on wild fruit and the flesh of monkeys that they shot with their rifles. Twice Trevithick nearly died - once he fell into the swollen Magdalena river but was rescued when a Venezuelan lassoed him and another time he was attacked by an alligator. Eventually they stumbled out of the jungle, half-starved and bedraggled, on the coast of Colombia at Cartagena.

It was here that the two great steam pioneers of the 19th century met - George Stephenson had been engaged by the Colombian Mining Association and was working in the country. The younger man by a decade took pity on the great inventor and forwarded him £50 so that he could book a passage back to Britain via New York.

Trevithick landed in Cornwall on October 9th 1827. He had been away 11 years - he arrived back with no money, the clothes he stood up in, a gold watch, a compass and a pair of silver spurs. On paper he had the rights to a copper mountain in Caxatambo and an option on certain gold mines in Costa Rica. Once they had got their land legs (and Richard had reacquainted himself with his long-suffering wife and six children), Trevithick and Gerard set about the task of getting financial backers for their rather dubious South American business ventures. During the negotiations in London Trevithick was actually offered a cheque for £8,000 for his copper rights. But his impetuosity got the better of him and he fell out with the interested party and failed to clinch the deal. A friend asked him: "Why did you not pocket the cheque *before* you quarrelled?" to which he replied "I would sooner kick them downstairs!"

That was the end of making his fortune from South America. But still the ideas kept coming, and he would rush on to another scheme before bringing the first to fruition. This lack of patience and of persistence proved disastrous to his fame and fortune. One commentator wrote: 'Many lessons which experience had taught him had to be relearned by subsequent inventors, who bore off the laurels which he might have earned.'

During the last five years of his life the projects that he worked on included screw propellers for steam boats, the making of artificial ice, a new recoil gun carriage and apparatus for heating rooms. Which brings us to the last year of his life - 1833. In this year he was working on an invention at John Hall's foundry in Dartford and lodging in The Bull Inn in the town. He was suddenly taken ill and died. He not only had no money for the funeral, he still owed the innkeeper for his board and lodging. However, the workers at Hall's clubbed together to give him a decent funeral and these same men followed Trevithick on his last journey to the churchyard and he was buried in an unmarked grave. So one of the greatest inventors this country has ever seen is forever now in Kent, albeit without a headstone to record the exact spot.

Later, in 1888, a memorial window was erected in the north aisle of the nave of Westminster Abbey, next to the Brunel window and his name is remembered by an engineering scholarship at Manchester University and a triennial medal at the Institution of Civil Engineers.

Today there is a Trevithick Society which honours the great man and also remembers his two sons and two grandsons, also successful engineers (his grandson, Richard, designed and built Japan's first locomotive). The latter two spent many years in Japan setting up the Japanese railway network after the country opened up to the West in the second half of the 19th century.

Dared to Stand Up to Cromwell

SIR HENRY VANE (1613-1662)

Sir Henry Vane

Oliver Cromwell once got so exasperated with Sir Harry Vane that he cried out: "O Sir Harry Vane, Sir Harry Vane, the Lord deliver me from Sir Harry Vane!" With Cromwell's reputation for ruthlessness, this *cri de coeur* could easily have been the death sentence for the man from Fairlawne, near Shipbourne, as it had been five centuries earlier when another head of state, Henry II had said of Thomas à Becket: "Who will rid me of this turbulent priest?" Four knights murdered Thomas in Canterbury Cathedral but Sir Harry escaped with his life this time, although he was to die on the scaffold several years later. But the altercation marked the end of his friendship with England's ruler. What Sir Harry had done was to speak out in a forthright way with the courage of his convictions and without fear of the consequences. Along with his freedom from corruption, these qualities made him one of the most pre-eminent politicians of the turbulent years when Britain was wracked by civil war and then ruled for just over a decade by someone other than a monarch.

Henry Vane was born in early 1613, into a distinguished Kent family (earlier called Fane) which had originated from Hadlow. Henry Fane, the first of the family to be involved in national affairs, took part in Sir Thomas Wyatt's rebellion against the marriage of Mary Tudor to Philip II of Spain in 1554 and was MP for the Cinque Ports. His son was a military commander under Elizabeth I, while his grandson, Henry Vane the Elder, was a wealthy courtier and ambassador in the court of James I. It was the elder Vane who sold the family lands at Hadlow and bought estates in Durham and Essex and at Fairlawne in Kent, between the villages of Plaxtol and Shipbourne.

Henry Vane the Younger was probably not born in Kent but at a family house north of the Thames as he was baptised on 26th May 1613 at the church of Debden, near Newport in Essex. He went to Westminster School and indulged himself in the good things of life (or 'inclined to the vanities of the world', as he described it), coming from a wealthy and privileged family as he did. But his life changed at 15 when he converted to Puritanism; he renounced his former life and lifestyle as 'sinful'. He went on to Magdalen College, Oxford. His reputation as his own man began there. Instead of taking the oath of allegiance at the matriculation ceremony wearing a student's gown as was customary, he insisted on wearing an ordinary cloak.

After university, with his father's help and connections, he went to study in Geneva and in 1631 spent time in Vienna with the English ambassador, where he perfected his French, the language of diplomacy in those days. His strict religious beliefs were also making life difficult for him when he returned to court in England; for two years he did not take Holy Communion for he could get no one to administer it to him standing. He refused to compromise even though several bishops tried to talk to him and persuade him to conform.

In 1635, with the king's permission, he sailed for the New World where religious tolerance was practiced. Many of these early colonists were a pretty motley crew - titled wasters, debtors, convicts seeking a last chance as well as merchant adventurers and ministers of the church - Sir Francis Bacon even described the settlers of Virginia as 'the scum of the earth.' So the young and serious Henry Vane, with spoke excellent French and had had some experience of diplomacy, stood out from the other colonists.

He arrived in Boston on 6th October on board the *Abigail* and was received with open arms as 'a young gentleman of excellent parts and one who had forsaken the honours of the court to enjoy the ordinances of Christ in their purity.'

The following year, 1636, he became a freeman of the colony at the beginning of March and by the end of the same month the colonists elected him their governor. But immediately there were problems - war with the Pequot Indians, unruly sailors on shore leave, religious disagreements among the different churches, factions bickering over real and imagined wrongs. It seemed that Vane was out of his depth. He was publicly rebuked by one colonist who said "before he (Vane) came to Massachusetts the churches were at peace" and that he should "humbly consider his youth and short experience of the things of God, and to beware of peremptory conclusions which he was very apt unto."

Unquestionably he made many mistakes, but the greatest mistake was made by the colonists themselves, when, out of deference to birth and rank, they elevated a callow newcomer into a position of authority. In 1637 John Winthrop and his faction out-manoeuvred Vane and his supporters in elections for magistrates and he used this setback to make his excuses and leave. On 3rd August he set sail for England, a little older and a lot wiser.

Back in England Vane was appointed treasurer to the Navy thanks to his father dropping a word in the right ear. In 1640, Henry the Younger was knighted and upon his marriage to Frances Wray in the same year his father made over to him the estate at Fairlawne. He was also elected MP for Hull and sat in the famous Short and Long Parliaments, which preceded the Civil War. Once in the Commons, he approached debating and law making with his customary zeal. One contemporary writer describes that Henry 'was usually so engaged for the public in the house and several committees from early in the morning to very late at night, that he had scarce any leisure to eat his bread, converse with his nearest relations, or at all mind his family affairs.' But Sir Henry Vane the Younger's main claim to fame was that he played a leading role in the parliamentary campaign against Charles I. In effect, there was a single issue - who should have the sovereign power in the kingdom, the king or the people? For Vane, there was no question - the people were the source of all just power.

Vane was a leading advocate of the abolition of bishops and along with his father, Henry the Elder, and others, was instrumental in securing the impeachment of Charles I's chief minister, the Earl of Strafford, who was tried and beheaded, having been found guilty of proposing to use Irish troops to suppress Charles's parliamentary opponents. Needless to say, both Vanes were dismissed from the king's service by testifying against Charles's chief minister. Once the breach between king and parliament had opened into war, the younger Vane went to Scotland to negotiate the Solemn League and Covenant with the Presbyterians. He seems to have learnt from his unfortunate experiences in America and used considerable subtlety to achieve a favourable agreement. Back in

England, he took over the leadership of the parliamentary party in the House of Commons on the death of John Pym - he was now a figure of national importance.

While this was going on, Vane the Elder was trying to mediate between the Royalists and the Parliamentarians. He had been elected as an MP from Kent but he withdrew later on in favour of his cousin, Sir Roger Twysden of East Peckham. In 1643 he called a meeting of the county committee at Fairlawne to try to bring both sides in Kent together; but it was already too late.

Young Henry was trying to do the same thing on a national scale by travelling to Newport on the Isle of Wight and negotiating face to face with the king, who was a prisoner there in 1648 - this was strongly opposed by some of his more hot-headed colleagues. Cromwell himself was intent on settling the matter once and for all and actively pressed for the king's prosecution. When he was found guilty, Cromwell had no hesitation in signing the death warrant, something that the young Henry bitterly opposed and refused to do. Up until then Cromwell and the younger Henry had been close personal friends, they even had nicknames for each other - Vane addressed Cromwell as 'Brother Fountain' and Cromwell addressed Vane as 'Brother Heron'. But this incident signalled the beginning of the end of their friendship.

Relationships between the two of them got worse when Cromwell refused to accept that the Navy was as important as Vane claimed. Henry had been given special responsibility in the Council of State, which now governed England, for taking charge of foreign affairs and defence.

The final break between Cromwell and Vane came when the Protector dissolved the Long Parliament in 1653 and decided to rule with a nominated rather than elected assembly. Henry protested in the House: "This is not honest, yea it is against morality and common honesty," which prompted Cromwell to make his prayer for deliverance.

As can be imagined in a man of such strong conviction, Henry Vane wanted no part in an administration run by a man who appeared to be intoxicated by power and he refused an invitation to serve in the new nominated 'Parliament of the Saints'. Vane retired from public life and busied himself in theology and wrote such tracts as *The Retired Man's Meditations of the Mystery and Power of Godliness*.

But he refused to fade away and attacked the autocratic nature of the government and called for such safeguards as a written constitution. For this seditious activity he was sent into exile on the Isle of Wight from where he wrote to Cromwell and told him he was head of the Army under the legislative authority of the people represented in parliament, but nothing more, and that a Protector must be simply a chief magistrate not an imitation of a king. All of this, of course, did nothing to endear him to his erstwhile friend.

With Cromwell's death in 1658, Henry came back once more into public life. He hoped that at last a pure republic, which he longed to see, might be established. But his fellow countrymen, having experimented with a secular head of state and been disappointed, were in favour of the monarch returning.

Henry may have been involved in a last attempt to save England from monarchy in the last days of the Commonwealth. A plot was devised whereby Prince Charles and his brother James (the future Charles II and James II) were to be brought over to England and lodged at a house in Westenhanger near Hythe. Here they would be set upon and assasinated. It is not clear how far Henry was a party to this improbable scheme, but certainly he remained implacably opposed to the restoration of the monarchy. And after the Restoration he was one of the few men exempted by parliament from the general pardon of rebels - he was tried and despite a spirited defence, which he conducted himself, he was found guilty of treason. He was taken to Tower Hill on June 14th 1662 to be executed. He mounted the scaffold and 'bore himself with great composure and cheerfulness and seemed rather a looker-on than the person concerned in the execution'. His dying speech was interrupted three times by drums and trumpets but he endeavoured to justify the cause for which he suffered. 'In all things,' records Samuel Pepys who was moved to tears, 'he appeared the most resolved man that ever died in that manner' and believed 'that the king had lost more than he had gained by his execution.'

Be that as it may, Charles II did release his body to his family (his eldest son had predeceased him in 1660 but there remained six more sons and seven daughters). He was brought back to Kent and laid to rest in the vault of Shipbourne Church. He was joined there, in 1679, when his wife Lady Frances died. During the last 17 years of her life she had maintained non-conformist services at Fairlawne as a mark of respect for her husband, despite considerable persecution.

As if to make up for the little time he had spent in Kent when alive, Sir Henry Vane is in the county now and forever after, in body and spirit. His ghost, with his head under his arm, is supposed to haunt the yew walks at Fairlawne.

* * *

To India, in half the time

Thomas Waghorn (1800-1850)

On a map of Europe and Asia, draw a pencil line from England on the top left to India on the bottom right. And that would be more or less the logical route, travelling from one country to the other, wouldn't it? But it wasn't until Thomas Waghorn came along. The conventional route - almost three times as long - was the sea route right round the Cape of Good Hope which added two more sides to the triangle. Thomas Waghorn changed all this, in the teeth of hostile opposition but losing his fortune and his health along the way.

Thomas Waghorn was born on June 20th 1800. His father was a Rochester butcher, whose shop was in the High Street, opposite the Mitre Hotel where Horatio Nelson once stayed in 1793. In 1812, at the age of 12, young Thomas became a midshipman at Chatham and served under Captain Wilson in HMS *Bahama*. In 1817, he passed his examinations for a commissioned rank, the youngest midshipman ever to do so. But it was a time when the Royal Navy was laying off men. The Napoleonic Wars were over and there were no more service jobs to be had.

Waghorn was not a man to give up easily and he joined the *Indiaman* on the Thames and sailed for Calcutta as third mate. In 1819, he joined the Bengal Marine Pilot Service and spent the next five years on the Hooghly River.

Upon the outbreak of the First Burmese War in 1824, Waghorn volunteered for active service and was given command of the East India Company's cutter, *Matchless*. He took part in five battles and was wounded in the thigh. Fighting conditions in the jungle were appalling and some four-fifths of the

Thomas Waghorn

British forces perished - from disease as much as from the fighting. Waghorn survived but his health suffered and his experiences there probably shortened his life.

During the war, his imagination had been fired by the possibilities of steam power (a combination of steam and sail) and he'd watch with wonder the performance of a river steamer, the *Enterprise*. His enthusiasm was catching and he managed to persuade the Calcutta merchants that steam navigation around the Cape was feasible.

He also considered steam passages up the Red Sea but was horrified to learn that coal at Suez was a prohibitive £20 a ton. However, he discovered that this could be reduced to about £4 a ton by having the coal carried by camels from Cairo to Suez.

Eventually the Calcutta merchants sent Waghorn home to see the East India Company and to convert them to his ideas. In Britain, he toured various cities, giving speeches on the benefits of steam. After 18 months, he gained an ally in Lord Ellenborough, president of the Indian Control Board, who commissioned him to travel to India with despatches - via Egypt and the Red Sea. He was instructed to bring back a reply from Bombay within three months - the time taken by the fastest ships via the Cape, for the outward voyage alone.

Waghorn left London on October 28th 1829 and established a record by reaching Trieste in only nine days. But there were to be no more records this trip. The promised steamer which was to meet him at Suez and take him through the Red Sea did not arrive and he had to travel by open boat from Suez to Jeddah. The crew were mutinous and he was forced to keep a loaded pistol permanently pointing in their direction.

At Jeddah, he managed to get a vessel of the Bombay Marine to land him at Bombay on March 21st 1830. He had lost 23 days waiting about between Cairo and Jeddah. However, he had made the journey and was convinced that this was the right route to India. From then on, he abandoned his advocacy of the Cape route. In the same month, the steamship passage from Bombay to Aden was inaugurated.

Waghorn took his enthusiasm home with him to London but had difficulty finding anyone with whom to share it. The post office was reluctant to change its established route. And although he received the thanks of the merchants in London and India, he could get no official backing from the government. He wrote pamphlets and addressed meetings and in 1834 gave evidence to a parliamentary committee, set up to investigate steam navigation to India.

During home visits, Waghorn spent a lot of time with his family in

Holborough, a hamlet near the village of Snodland in Kent. When he married, he too set up a home there. Locals often witnessed his bursts of temper and his obsession with punctuality which caused him to race everywhere on his horse.

Henry Smetham, a Strood author, recalled how one night on his way home late, Waghorn found the turnpike gate at the junction of North Street and High Street, Strood, closed. Nothing daunted, he urged his spirited horse to jump over the gate with the chaise still attached. It resulted in the death of the horse.

On another occasion, Waghorn arrived at the turnpike gate in Caxton Road near Temple Place to find the gateman had gone to bed. For some minutes, Waghorn shouted and screamed until the unfortunate gatekeeper arrived. When he did, Wahgorn punched him and knocked him down. Later, filled with remorse, Waghorn sent his assistant, Samuel Dove of Rochester, to pay the gateman a guinea. The gateman is supposed to have said: 'You tell your gov'nor he can damn well knock me down every time he passes if he give me a quid each time that he does it.' (Dove actually became so nervous through Waghorn's behaviour and fast driving that he left his service to become a Customs officer).

Author Smetham tells another story about how Waghorn got his favourite brand of Chinese green tea. As Waghorn's carriage sped past the tea shop at the same time each day, the shopkeeper had to toss a packet of tea into the carriage, which neither stopped or even slowed down. 'If the package was not there, the custom was lost'.

Waghorn travelled back to Egypt in a private capacity - in his words, 'with a sort of official stigma upon my sanity'. For three years, he lived as an Arab and supervised the building of eight stations between Cairo and Suez. He also set up hotels at each end and one in Alexandria. The great Pasha Mehemet guaranteed a safe passage along the route - an arrangement that was honoured even during hostilities with the British.

In 1839, Waghorn was invited to join the Earl of Munster and a party of officers from Bombay to London. They made the journey in 35 days, bringing Bombay 55 days nearer to London. Confident that he would now be entrusted with the mail, Waghorn formed a company, Waghorn & Co. But under pressure from the French, still the British government proved obdurate. The post continued to go via the Cape.

Waghorn reverted to his original trans-European route to Trieste. But even in this the government ran a competing service. Waghorn then made improvements along the route. He introduced horse-drawn carriages rather than camels along the desert part of the route and small steamers along the Nile.

However, Waghorn could no longer compete with the government against him. He had invested all his money into his great schemes and his funds had gone. But small rewards did at last come his way. For a quarter of a century he had been a (retired) midshipman. Now the Admiralty promoted him to lieutenant.

Waghorn was of course delighted with his promotion but it didn't change his circumstances. With little money and broken in health, he retired to Malta. The government gave him a pension of £200 a year and the East India Company matched this pound for pound. But even this was only enough to pay his creditors. He returned home on Christmas day 1849 and died on January 6th 1850 in a back street house in Islington. His body was brought to Snodland, Kent, for burial.

His widow was left an annual government pension of £40 and another £50 from the East India Company.

In 1888, a large crowd gathered for the unveiling of a statue to Waghorn in Chatham. It is still there, below the New Road bridge over Railway Street. It was supposed to be pointing to the overland routes to the east but this is geographically incorrect. Local humorists say that Waghorn's outstretched finger simply guides people to the near-by public lavatories.

Others recognised the value of his work. Ferdinand de Lesseps, builder of the Suez Canal, erected a larger-than-life-size head and shoulders statue at Port Tewfik, at the entrance to the Canal. But sadly, political events intervened: it was smashed to pieces in the Suez crisis in 1956.

All the Charm of Royalty and Persuasion of an All-In Wrestler

DR DORRIT ARMITAGE WATERFIELD (1897-1982)

Dorrit Waterfield was an unconventional but very popular GP who practiced from her home, Little Grange, just outside Lamberhurst and, at first, from a small surgery on the Hastings Road and then larger premises on the Lower Green Road in Pembury. She spent her time helping other people, trying to make the physically and mentally unwell get better, or at least lead a more rewarding life. Dorrit was never really off duty - when not at her GP's surgery, or at the Kent & Sussex hospital in Tunbridge Wells where she worked as a part-time anaesthetist, she was a founding member, volunteer and, for several years, the director of the Tunbridge Wells branch of The Samaritans. Even at home she was caring for people - she would let people stay for long or short periods. Her house guests needed time and space and quiet to get their minds and bodies back in shape.

Born at Arnold House (a prep school) in Hastings on May 28th 1897, Dorrit Armitage Waterfield was the daughter of a nurse, Mary (whose maiden name was Armitage), and a preparatory school master, Harry, who later became the head of the Temple Grove School, Eastbourne. Dorrit and her younger sister Kathleen were pupils at this all boys school, but her father, who had been ordained in 1901, 'recruited' a few other girls to keep them company. Surrounded by books and in a learning environment, from an early age she helped with the teaching in the schools where her father worked and she developed a love of English and the classics, which would never leave her.

At the beginning of the last century, 'Gals', as she called her peers, were not encouraged to enter universities, so she made her point by getting a place at the London Hospital Medical School. She knew nothing of the natural sciences, and only had her mother's *Gray's Anatomy* to teach her the basics of her chosen profession, but her faith and intuitive feeling was in people, not narrow academic disciplines.

By working hard at the bookish stuff, she managed to qualify for membership of the Royal College of Surgeons (MRCS) and received a licence to practice from the Royal College of Physicians (LRCP) in 1924. She became the house anaesthetist at the London Hospital and was appointed house physician (despite considerable opposition from male colleagues) to Lord Dawson of Penn, the senior consultant at the London and other hospitals, as well as physician to King George V.

Some of the pupils in her father's school could not go home for the holidays as their parents were in the far-flung corners of the British Empire, so these 'sons of Empire' had to be farmed out to family and friends. This is how the Waterfield family came to Little Grange in the High Weald just south of Tunbridge Wells. It was a big rambling house and so could accommodate some of the boys during the school holidays.

Harry gave up the headship to Temple Grove in 1935 but remained as school chaplain when it moved to Heron's Ghyll; he also served as the private chaplain to Lord Camden in the estate chapel near Lamberhurst. Dorrit's father was blind in one eye and would often, much to his passengers' consternation, drive along the country lanes on the wrong side of the road because he could see better! Some also said: "Like father, like daughter," as Dorrit put a lot of faith in her car horn, more so than in the Highway Code and reckoned that everyone knew her vehicle anyway. One of her patients, Dick Miles, a farmer who lives at Fletchers' Farm in Pembury, remembers her Standard Eight motorcar and her behind the wheel as "a bloody good driver, if a little fast." She only once had an accident - hitting a tractor head on in a country lane. "She also had very cold hands," recalls Dick, "and, surprisingly, for someone so forthright, was not a very good public speaker. She didn't like public holidays and often volunteered to work on them."

In 1929 Dorrit left London and came to live in Little Grange, between Pembury and Lamberhurst, and set up practice as the first woman GP in the area. At first she did her rounds on a bicycle before graduating to a motorbike. Even back in the 1930s the part of the A21 that went almost in front of her house was a notoriously dangerous piece of road for traffic with many sweeping blind bends and she frequently complained that the press only photographed her bottom up attending car crashes. But much of her practice was looking after the people who lived in the hamlets and farms around her home and she would dispense medicine for her patients from Little Grange and perform minor surgery on a marble topped washstand.

During the Second World War she frequently went back up to London to offer her services during the Blitz. She would drive up with a mattress tied to the roof rack to ward off the bombs. During this time Little Grange was opened as a nursing home for old ladies and she used the two-acre garden to grow vegetables and so help the war effort. She was particularly well known for her tomatoes. One of the secrets of her horticultural prowess was not wasting anything. When Dick Miles's wife Frances had her first son, she asked if she could take the placenta home. Being a farmer's wife, Frances, was not at all squeamish and said she could - Dorrit dug it into the ground around her tomatoes. Pembury Horticultural Society has a cup named after her in recognition of her great gardening skills.

Dr Dorrit Armitage Waterfield

"She was a very strong woman, very forthright in her opinions" remembers Frances. "You didn't disagree with her. But she didn't always get it right. When I had my second childbirth I knew I was carrying twins, but Dorrit insisted there was only one. When the second arrived five minutes later she was very apologetic. She was also very good for the local community, insisting, for example, that the local Pembury Women's Institute have an evening meeting especially for the young wives with children - she said they needed to get out of the house and that their husbands could jolly well baby-sit at least one evening a month."

Another patient, Joan Chapman, wife of the former editor of *The Kent & Sussex Courier* remembers her GP with affection. "After my first baby I lost a lot of weight and Dr Waterfield put me on a fattening diet; all it managed to do was put on half a pound. After my second baby I put on three and a half stone and I asked Dr Waterfield why that had happened. She could not really explain it and just said it was due to my metabolism. I then said: 'If I have a third baby, will I lose weight again?' She admitted she didn't know and definitely could not say that I would, because she did not want to find a baby on her doorstep if I didn't!"

Because she spent so much time in the garden, she would not change when she was called out to a patient out of hours. If called out at night, Betty Paxman, her house keeper, would heat a glass of milk for her before she went out into the dark - she would arrive at a farmhouse or cottage, stub out her cigarette, and go in wearing corduroy trousers with string hanging out of the pocket, a hessian apron and a poke bonnet.

When, in later life, her faculties were diminishing, she would blame her stethoscope for not working properly when she couldn't hear the heart beat properly. Eventually she wore a hearing aid which she sometimes had trouble with when it let off a piercing scream - most memorably twice, once in a coroner's court and the other time at Glyndebourne. But it could also be used to her advantage - she was underwhelmed by the attempts to modernise the spoken parts of a the Church of England service and she would turn her hearing aid down on occasions in church and recite the old versions of favourite prayers and psalms.

She also needed glasses and would have them on a string around her neck when they weren't on the bridge of her nose. Frances Miles remembers one day she was on her knees in her garden cutting the edge of the lawn with hedge clippers and accidentally cut the strings - when she had finished she couldn't for the life of her remember where she had put her glasses and only found them a day later in the garden where she had snipped them off. Keys were the bane of her life - to the mantra of "Wait a minute. Wait a minute", she would always be riffling through her voluminous handbag searching for them. They turned up in the most unlikely places, once in the kitchen refrigerator - Dorrit swore a poltergeist was responsible.

Dorrit took a great interest in alcoholics, many of whom had had a very traumatic time in the war and had serious psychiatric illnesses as a result. Little Grange was a haven and a halfway house for such people and she did her best to rehabilitate them. Many times the police would phone her up and say that somebody who claimed to be an ex-RAF pilot was drunk, dishevelled and incapable of rational conversation except for a slurred "Doctor Waterfield" and "Little Grange." No matter what the time of day or night she would drive to a police station or a call box and pick up one of her 'boys' and take them back to her home.

She helped others besides ex-serviceman. John Clements was a resident at Little Grange for five years. He remembers her with affection and gratitude. "Dirty, drunk or twice her size, it was all the same to her. When all else failed, she sat on us with a cup of tea in one hand and a hypodermic in the other. She dispensed advice, discipline, and medicines with all the charm of Royalty and persuasion of an all-in wrestler. Psychiatric care requires enormous skill, patience and a sense of humour, which she possessed in abundance."

John recalls one occasion at Little Grange when the doctor had to sew up a farm worker who had been badly gored by a boar. Once the patient had been seen to, she calmly took out some more sewing and started mending saying: "I may as well while I'm in the mood."

Her unconventional approach was recognised by her medical colleagues. Dr Donald Hunter was a consultant physician at the London Hospital in the 1920s and in later life edited a *Textbook of the Practice of Medicine* and presented Dr Waterfield with a copy. On the frontispiece he wrote 'To Dorrit who knows lots of things in clinical medicine which have never been written in books.'

Dorrit owned a shotgun and would happily pot rabbits and squirrels from her bedroom window. Once in later life a friend was massaging her when a rabbit was spotted in the garden - she jumped up in her underwear and ran to get her gun; but her aim was not as good as it used to have been and all she managed was to knock over a gladiolus. Roadkill was also considered fair game for the cooking pot - once she picked up a pheasant on the roadside and thought it best to gut it there and then. This she did with consummate skill with a pair of nail scissors.

In 1960, her nephew Peter Waterfield joined her as a GP at Little Grange and 12 years later she made over the practice to him. But she continued to help out and worked a seven to eight hour 'part-time' day. In 1979 she reached her Golden Jubilee in practice as the local GP and her grateful patients presented her with a garden seat. She thought the deputation had come for surgery and greeted them with stethoscope and prescription pad. When the practice moved from its premises in Lower Green Road to a newly-built surgery nearby it was named Waterfield House in tribute to her memory. She died in a nursing home in Tunbridge Wells of cancer on April 7th 1982 at the age of 84 and her ashes were buried in the grave of her parents at Lamberhurst church.

During the cremation service, which was packed, John Clements had a vision of her as one of her fellow Samaritans' was reading the committal. "I saw Dorrit at the Pearly Gates, struggling with her hand bag and telling St Peter: 'Wait a minute. Wait a minute.' Then with a winning smile, she treated him as all foolish males, walking straight past him and smelling his breath. He, of all people, understood a fellow Saint, a life meant for living and a humanity all about people."

✳ ✳ ✳

Prophet, Lover, Socialist, and Writer of Genius

HERBERT GEORGE WELLS (1866-1946)

HG Wells, born in Bromley, Kent, is remembered as an outstanding writer in three genres, a prophet of the future, a socialist and a lover of beautiful women.

At first glance, he was no Adonis but rather an unpretentious little man with a squeaky voice. Look closer and you'd have seen a powerful round skull, jutting lips beneath a narrow moustache and brilliant pale blue eyes that could sparkle with fun or hostility.

Was it then his genius that drew women to him? Michael Foot, author of the recent biography, *The History of Mr Wells,* thinks it was both mind and body. And there were many who fell for that fatal combination. Wells himself described his series of affairs as 'escapades of a Don Juan among the intelligentsia'. A woman novelist went some way to explaining his attractiveness to women. She wrote: 'He always seemed nearer and more sympathetic than other men. He understood those enchanting gestures which send a spark to the very heart of a woman'.

One of his most important relationships was with Rebecca West, writer, novelist, critic and described by contemporaries as a libertine. She gave birth to Wells' son, Anthony, in 1909. Rebecca was the most articulate of all his loves. She challenges the assertion that HG was simply a womaniser who loved and let go. She writes: ... 'rather than discard women, he was more often discarded himself ... [but] the women who left him all felt enduring affection for him and were his domestic friends in his old age'.

Like Charles Dickens, Wells (whose family knew him as Bertie) began life in very humble surroundings. He was born on September 21st 1866, in a shabby bedroom over a shop, at 47 High Street, Bromley, Kent. His mother, a former housekeeper, was 44. The house had no running water and the only lavatory was a cesspool in the yard, a short distance from a well and rain water tank.

The dilapidated downstairs shop had an almost indecipherable sign with the words Joseph Wells Emporium. For sale were cheap crockery and cricketing paraphernalia. Cricketing gear because Bertie's father Joseph was a professional cricketer, who on June 26th 1862 had created a record by bowling four Sussex batsmen in successive balls. And it was his income as a cricketer that financed a number of very cheap fee-paying schools for Bertie.

One was the Bromley Academy, at which the prospectus claimed, he could learn, 'Geography Sacred and Secular, Arithmetic (logically) and Plain and Ornamental Writing.' The last of these schools was Morley's Academy, also in the High Street and not far from his father's emporium. On the whole, the education was very basic but Bertie constantly visited the local literary institute, where he read omnivorously.

H G Wells

When he was 14, his father broke a leg and the resultant limp meant he was unable to pursue his career as a cricket coach. The shop was hardly making any money at all and they decided to abandon it. The family broke up and Bertie's mother went back to her old job as housekeeper at Up Park, in Sussex.

Bertie's two elder brothers had already become journeymen drapers and Bertie's mother arranged that he too should follow suit. He was apprenticed to Rodgers and Denyer in Windsor. He hated the job and very soon his employers were as pleased to be rid of him as he was to leave. In his autobiography, Wells says, 'I was not refined enough to become a draper'.

By a stroke of luck, he was then offered the position of pupil-teacher at Alfred Williams' school in Wookey, Somerset. This post also proved to be temporary and after a short spell again stayed with his mother at Up Park. These false starts continued when he was once more apprenticed to a draper, this time in Southsea. He laboured here two years, hating every minute of it. Then, another lucky break, he was offered the position of under-master at Midhurst Grammar School. At first his mother refused to allow him to leave his job as she had already paid £40 of his apprenticeship premium. But Bertie threatened suicide and his mother relented.

Midhurst changed the course of his life. He did some classroom teaching but also studied hard as a pupil. He passed his exams so successfully, he was offered a studentship with a maintenance grant of £1 a week at the Normal School (later Royal College) of Science, South Kensington.

He did well at first, under T H Huxley (who he always said was his best teacher) and passed his first year biology with flying colours. However, with other teachers in physics and geology, he became lax and it was said he spent more time in the library than in the laboratory. He was also getting about more and had developed new outside interests. Chief of these was socialism and most of his nights were spent at meetings, addressed by the likes of William Morris and Bernard Shaw. There was another new interest too. It was while he was at the Normal School that, in 1886, he met his cousin Isabel, to whom he was immensely attracted.

Wells next taught at the Holt Academy at Wrexham where his health took a disastrous turn. During a game of football, he permanently damaged a kidney. He then developed tuberculosis with haemorrhages. This meant convalescing with his mother at Up Park but with plenty of opportunity to use the house's well stocked library.

His next teaching post was at Henley House School, Kilburn, kept by the father of A A Milne. In 1890, he sat for his BSc and gained a first in zoology and a second in geology.

A year later, as a full time tutor earning £4 a week, he married his cousin, Isabel, at Wandsworth on October 31st 1891 and immediately ran into marital problems. These were mostly caused by sexual inexperience which wasn't helped by Isabel's belief that lovemaking was a sexual outrage against women! In frustration, he seduced one of Isabel's friends, discovering for the first time that sex could be highly enjoyable.

In 1892, he began a relationship with Amy Catherine Robbins (always known as Jane), one of his students at the Tutorial College, and eloped with her the following year, when he was 27. In 1895, when divorce proceedings were finalised, he married Jane.

In 1899, HG took Jane for a tandem ride through Sussex and Kent. They travelled along the south coast, but by the time they reached Sandgate, where they had booked rooms, Wells became so ill that he doubted if he would live. He had a soaring temperature, haemorrhage of the lungs and an abscess on a kidney. What could they do? They were in a strange town and knew nobody.

Then Wells remembered a doctor friend - Dr Hick, Medical Officer for Health for Romney. A telegram was sent: 'Am ill. Can you take me in?' The doctor and his family responded generously and put up Wells and his wife in their home and in five weeks the patient was on the mend.

He was then advised to convalesce on the South Coast, on gravely soil, in a sheltered spot. Jane took temporary lodgings at Beach Cottages, Sandgate. Every day, she went out looking for houses while her husband spent the mornings in bed and basked in the sun during the afternoon.

HG's health improved enormously but Jane had not yet found a suitable house for them. So they moved to better accommodation a few houses away. Creatively, the time wasn't wasted for although the body was stricken, the mind was alert. The future *Kipps* came into his mind at this time and as his health improved, he was able to finish *Love and Mr Lewisham,* the novel on which he was working before his illness. Another book written during this period was *The First Men in the Moon.*

He began to feel much better and attributed his improvement to the climate of Sandgate and Folkestone. He wrote: 'This place (plus Folkestone) is the most habitable place I've ever been in. For an elderly invalid (as I am practically) it is incomparable'.

Jane had been busy searching for a house but had found none that suited their requirements. So HG decided to have one built. Spade House came into being towards the end of 1900, a graceful modern house with sea views and sweeping lawns. It was his home for some ten years. One of the first novels to emerge from this period was *The Sea Lady,* the story of a mermaid, published in 1902.

HG was not short of company in Spade House and entertained a circle of other writers, some living locally, which included Henry James, Joseph Conrad, Ford Madox Ford, George Gissing and Arnold Bennett. They had long discussions of what made up the modern novel. Wells maintained that he wanted to show what made up English society and he aimed to show his characters within that society. He called it 'Social Comparative Anatomy'.

HG was now writing well and beginning to reap the benefits. He had published a number of science fiction stories and had seen these labelled as Wellsian. These included *The Time Machine* (1895), *The Invisible Man* (1897), and - much later - *The Shape of Things to Come* (1933). As well as a good income, they made Wells' reputation as a prophet.

With uncanny accuracy, he anticipated tanks, war in the air, the atomic bomb and 'the war of 1940'. As recently as 1965, the Russian newspaper,

Pravda, credited 'this great English writer' as being the first person to imagine the concept of the Sputnik. In 1909, before any aircraft had even crossed the Channel, he had created fictional 'victorious aeroplanes sweeping down, dropping explosives and incendiaries'. People forgot about his misses such as the rejection of the idea of a submarine. Another was the First World War. He wrote: 'At the bottom of my heart I did not feel and believe that it would be allowed to happen'.

After the Wellsian romances came the so called 'real' novels. These included *The Wheels of Chance* (1896), *Love and Mr Lewisham* (1900), *Kipps,* and *Tono-Bungay.* In total Wells wrote over 100 books and at the height of his powers, enjoyed an income of over £50,000 a year - a fortune in turn-of-the-century Britain.

In 1910, the Wells family left Spade House, although a 1911 local guide book described the locality as 'The H G Wells coast'. HG felt he needed to be nearer London and the world of publishers and journalism. His spirit was restless and it seems he couldn't bear to be in one place too long. After a tour of the Continent, they moved to 17 Church Row, Hampstead. HG also took what he described as a minute flat in Camden Street.

After the First World War, he again changed the genre in which he worked. It was his encyclopaedic phase and included such tomes as *The Outline of History* (1920), *The Science of Life* (1931) and *The Work, Wealth and Happiness of Mankind* (1932). It was said that these alone would have established his name as a substantial writer.

Towards the end of his life, HG tried his hand at writing for the screen. In 1936 he wrote the script for *The Man Who Could Work Miracles* and the epic *Things to Come.* He also went in for radio, hoping that the microphone would compensate for his squeaky voice - but he never became a broadcasting personality.

During the Second World War, he lived at 13 Hanover Terrace, Regents Park, defying the Blitz to do its worst and putting out incendiaries with the help of two servants. Several blasts blew in his front door and apparently on these occasions HG slept through it all upstairs.

Twice he stood, unsuccessfully, as Labour candidate for the University of London and in July 1945, left what was his final sickbed to vote for Labour.

On the morning of August 13th 1946, he rang for the nurse but when she arrived, found he had nothing to ask her. He told her to go away and in the ten minutes she was absent, HG died. He was short of his 80th birthday by 39 days. For a man who had made fortunes, his will was something of a surprise. His whole estate amounted to no more than £58,811.

HG had honorary degrees from various universities and submitted a doctoral thesis to the university of London to become D.Sc. But one honour always evaded him - to be a fellow of the Royal Society. In 1938, he wrote his own epitaph: 'He was clever but was not clever enough'.

There would have been many who disagreed. But perhaps George Orwell, writing in the *Manchester Evening News,* should be allowed the last say: 'No writer of our time, at any rate no English writer, has so deeply influenced his contemporaries as Wells. He was so big a figure, he has played so great a part in forming our picture of the world that in agreeing or disagreeing with his ideas we are apt to forget his purely literary achievements. In his own eyes it was a secondary, almost an unimportant thing. He had faults of intellect and of character, but very few writers have had less literary vanity'.

The Pride of Kent

FRANK WOOLLEY (1887-1978)

The Dictionary of National Biography has 'cricketer' as the first word in Frank Edward Woolley's entry. This sums up the Tonbridge man's life admirably. Between 1906 and his retirement from the professional game at the age of 51 in 1938, he scored 58,969 runs (second behind Sir Jack Hobbs who scored 61,237 in his career) in 979 first class matches. Woolley's total of runs included 145 centuries at an average 40.75. He also took 2,068 wickets for 19.85 runs each; and he held 1,018 catches, mainly fielding at slip, a record which remains unsurpassed. He shares with W G Grace the record of having made 1,000 runs or more 28 times, in his case, in successive seasons. Twelve of these times he reached 2,000, and in 1928, 3,352. He was Wisden's Cricketer of the Year in 1911 and was generally acknowledged to be the outstanding all-rounder of his age and deserved to be called 'the Pride of Kent'.

Frank was born in Tonbridge on May 27th 1887, the fourth and youngest son (he had no sisters) of Charles Woolley, a bicycle maker, and his wife Louise Lewis who came from Ashford. His home was above his father's shop at 72 High Street and out the back was the engineering workshop where the bicycles were made - at first boneshakers, then beautiful hand-enamelled models with pneumatic tyres. The workshop also provided something else. The four boys would chalk a wicket on the door and take it in turns to bat in front of it in the back yard. The two C's, Charlie and Claude, always played the two F's, Fred and Frank. A ball struck to two other doors scored two, a more distant door was four, and over the gates into Onley's stable yard was six.

The four boys were well known and popular in Tonbridge. Their father had built them a little yellow and black carriage, which was drawn by four cream-coloured goats. Charlie, the oldest brother, always insisted on taking the reins. Charlie was also to become a professional cricketer and later played for Gloucestershire and Northants and after that became an umpire.

Frank was good at all sports, and if a racquet or bat was involved he held it in his left hand. He also liked football and played for a local Tonbridge team. But it was cricket that appealed the most and he was lucky in that the Kent County team had its nursery school for budding talent in the town. Young Frank used to hang around the nursery and when he was 12, Colin Blythe, an established Kent player invited him to join in batting and bowling in the nets. By the age of 14, the lanky lad, six foot three, was taken on as one of the cricket nursery's ground staff. His height came from his mother - she was six feet tall. His winter work was in his father's engineering business and on Saturdays he played inside left for his soccer team.

In 1906, he played his first county game for Kent against Lancashire. It was an inauspicious first innings - he was out for a duck and only managed one wicket for 103 and missed three catches. But in the second innings he scored a fine 64. His third match was the stuff of storybook heroics. It was against Surrey at the Oval and the match was critical for Kent's championship aspirations. It was a low scoring match with Surrey out for 73 in their first innings, but they did better in the second innings, totalling 254. Woolley took five wickets in each innings. Kent's lead of 127 on the first innings, with Woolley contributing 72 having gone into bat at No 8, meant that they needed 128 to win. At 109 for 9, the young Woolley saw his side through to a notable victory by a single wicket by stroking the ball to the boundary.

In retirement, he recalled this nail-biting match. "In the whole of my career, I have never had such a half hour as that which followed. The crowd was swarming onto the ground. Somebody stole my bat (this was returned later) and whether in excitement or not I shall never know, but I got two proper whacks from an umbrella on my shoulders and back. Somebody pressed two sovereigns into my hand, and by the time I was able to reach the dressing room I hardly knew what I was doing. At the finish, probably in my hurry to escape, I actually got into my bath with one boot on."

Although his first season with Kent was not a full one, Frank still scored over 600 runs including his first century against Hampshire in his home town of Tonbridge and took over 40 wickets. The county side went on to take the championship, a feat they repeated again in 1909, 1910 and 1913. In 1911 they were runners-up to Warwickshire and third in 1912 and 1914. This pre-war era was outstanding for producing brilliant amateur cricketers, mainly by the universities. Woolley was learning the game and maturing in the company of such greats as Fry, Jessop, Prince Ranjitsinhji, Maclaren, Hirst, Rhodes, Jackson, Hobbs and Barnes.

It was during this golden age of cricket that Woolley started his Test career that was to last for 16 years and 64 Test matches, during which he scored five centuries and 3,283 runs at an average of 36. In 1909, he went to South Africa and played one match against a local team of 22 players, of whom all fielded! In 1911 he went on the tour to Australia, which England won four Tests to one. Frank's personal record for this tour included 305 not out against Tasmania; a total of 781 runs with an average of 55.78 and 17 wickets at a cost of 29.58.

At 27, in 1914, Frank was at the peak of his playing ability. He married in the same year, Sybil Fordham, daughter of an Ashford veterinary surgeon. This was a most happy marriage, which lasted nearly 50 years and produced a son and two daughters. But of course normal life came to an end with the declaration of war.

Frank Woolley

Woolley was astonished to be rejected when he first presented himself to join up - faulty eyesight and teeth. The latter are not generally regarded as essential to being a good cricketer, but the former certainly are. Hitting a ball travelling in your direction at more than 90 miles per hour and catching one, in the split second it takes to travel from bat to first slip, certainly requires good eyesight. Frank declared the examiner 'barmy' and tried again - the second time he was successful and found himself in the Royal Navy in the motor boat section of the Air Service, stationed first at Felixstowe and then in Scotland. His experience working in his father's engineering shop no doubt accounted for this secondment.

He may have had some practical knowledge of engines but he lacked sea going experience and understanding of tides. When his launch arrived in the Firth of Forth, he secured it with mooring ropes in the approved seamanlike manner. Next morning a crowd had gathered to inspect the vessel suspended ten feet above the water.

A happy outcome of the war, unusual in large families, was that Frank and his three brothers all survived. But not unscathed; Charlie had been badly wounded in Gallipoli and Claude was blown up in France by a shell that killed his friend, the Kent slow bowler Colin Blythe, who had first spotted Frank's talents. Claude was an invalid for the rest of his life.

After the cessation of hostilities, professional cricket returned and Frank resumed duty for Kent and England. Needless to say he was a bit rusty. His worst ever bowling spell came in one of the first matches, played in 1919. At the Oval Surrey needed 95 to win in 44 minutes, with a slight drizzle and the light extremely bad. Kent were bowling their 13th over by the time Hobbs hit the winning runs with 15 minutes to spare. Woolley was hit for 54 in six overs. But he was soon back to his old form and he took his one and only hat trick against Surrey in that same summer.

In 1923 he hit his highest score for Kent - 270 runs in 260 minutes against Middlesex at Canterbury. Woolley, in common with other fine hitters of the ball, especially enjoyed playing Somerset at Taunton where the river beside the ground was a tempting target. In 1924, John Daniel, the Somerset captain complained about 'that blasted Woolley' who had despatched no less than nine Somerset balls out of the ground to be lost in the drink.

Post-war the Test matches against the Australians brought a reversal of fortunes for England. Ironically in the losing 1921 series, Woolley probably played his finest Test. At Lords in the second Test, against the visitors' fastest bowlers, Gregory and McDonald, Woolley hit 95 in the first innings and 93 in the second. The rivalry between the two teams was as keen as ever. One incident concerned an umpire's decision. The Australian bowler Warwick Armstrong was angry: "Nobody but a bloody Pom would have stood there." Implying that the batsman should have walked. Woolley with considerable hauteur replied: "Nobody but an Australian would have appealed in the first place."

In the autumn of his playing career, 1934, when he was 47, Woolley had a memorable season. When most cricketers were reaching for their slippers, he scored ten centuries for Kent, at an average time of around 107 minutes for each. His fastest was in fact 63 minutes against Nottinghamshire at Dover, which earned him a trophy and £100 in cash, for the fastest century of the season.

When he retired in 1938 (the season that for the first time during his long career he opened the batting for Kent), the eulogies were heart felt. Writers remarked how much he had been a joy to watch, playing an eminently straight bat, employing his long reach to full advantage, his timing of the ball approaching perfection. Another described him as the most graceful batsman of his day and that when you bowled to him there weren't enough fielders. For his services to cricket he was made an honorary member of the MCC and his old county Kent Cricket Club.

The great left-hander settled with his wife in Hildenborough and spent his time coaching at King's College, Canterbury. With the coming of the Second World War he moved to Cliftonville and served in Dad's Army, the Home Guard, initially armed with a broom handle, which had an outsized nail for offensive action.

Their only son, Richard, was lost at sea in the *Beaverford,* part of an ill-fated convoy protected only by *HMS Jervis Bay* which so gallantly sacrificed herself to the German U-boats to gain time for many of the ships to escape, but not, sadly, the ship in which Frank and Sybil's son was serving. Whilst on holiday recovering from this sad news, their Cliftonville home was destroyed by a stray bomb from a lone raider.

After the war the Woolleys lived in a flat in Tunbridge Wells but after his wife Sybil died in 1962, Frank went to live with his youngest daughter at Longwick in Buckinghamshire where she had a riding stables. On his 80th birthday there was a celebratory dinner at the Great Danes Hotel at Hollingbourne where the main speakers were Edward Heath and Colin Cowdrey, the Kent and England captain.

His final years were spent in Chester, Nova Scotia, where he married Martha Wilson Morse, the widow of a major of the Royal Tank Corps. His life's innings came to an end in Canada on October 18th 1978 at the age of 91.

SELECTED BIBLIOGRAPHY

1. Richard Barham
Hemphry, Malcolm in *Kent Life* October 1962
Bootes, Alfred in *Kent Life* October 1964
Janes, Hurford in *Kent Life* April 1969
Pamphlet from Tappington Hall Farm, Denton
2. H E Bates
Bootes, Alfred in *Kent Life* January 1975
Davis, Pat in *Kent Life* January 1985
3. Benjamin Beal
Thanet Heritage Services, Margate Library *Benjamin Beale and the Invention of the Bathing Machine* 1937
Goodsall, Robert H *A Second Kentish Patchwork* 1968
Clarke, G E *Historic Margate* (reprint) 1979
4. Edmund Blunden
Hirai, Masao and Milward, Peter, ed. *Edmund Blunden - A Tribute from Japan* Kenkyusha
Barnes, John pamphlet *The Blunden Family and Yalding* 1988
Bootes, Alfred in *Kent Life*
Elliott, Christopher in *East Anglian Magazine* Vol 23 1964
Obituary in *The Times* January 21st 1974
Makino, Tadashi original material from Ito City Tourist Association
5. Betty Bolaine
Cousins, H S in *Bygone Kent* Vol 5, No 10
Life & History of Betty Bolaine pamphlet (third edition) published in Canterbury in 1880
6. Denys Bower
Eldridge, Mary *Beyond Belief* Whitworth Press 1996
Booklet from Chiddingstone Castle
7. Louis Brennan
Robinson H A in *Model Engineer* April 26th 1956
Graham R in *Aeronautical Journal* February 1973
Tomlinson, Norman in *Kent Life* October 1975
8. Joseph Conrad
Joyce, Arthur H in *Bygone Kent* Vol 11, No 9
Graham, Margaret in *Kent Life* May 1969
Tyler, Edward in *Kent Life* January 1983
9. Richard Dadd
Trial reported in Rochester Gazette August 6th 1844
Allderidge, Patricia in Sunday Times Magazine September 24th 1972
Bignell, Alan *Kent Murders* Countryside Books 1992
10. Charles Darwin

Moorehead, Alan *Darwin and the Beagle* Hamish Hamilton 1969
Meyer, Ronald P in *Kent Life* June 1973
Geere, Barbara and Anthony in *Kent Life* January 1993

11. Sir Humphrey Gilbert
Tyler, Lisa in *Journal of Kent Local History* September 1983
Hughes David T in *Bygone Kent* Vol 12, No 8

12. Charles Hamilton
Evans, Bill in *Kent Life* December 1978
Bond, Philip in *Kent Life* December 1991
Hall, Maurice *I Say You Fellows!*

13. William Harvey
Bishop C H *Some Folkestone Worthies*
Snow, Stephen in *Kent Life* May 1978

14. William Hazlitt
Fisher, Sylvia in *Kent Life* May 1983
Paulin, Tom in *The Independent Magazine* August 6th 1994

15. Dr Hewlett Johnson
Laxon, Colin in *Bygone Kent* Vol 6, No 3

16. John Latham
Harrison, James in *Kent Life* February 1969

17. Christopher Marlowe
Monograph: lecture by Professor Richard Proudfoot King's College, London 1993
Coates, Stephen in *Kent Life* February 1986
Edwards, Sue in *Kent Life* May 1993

18. Arthur Mee
Laming, Barbara in *Kent Life* July 1975
Quinton, Anthony in *Times Literary Supplement* July 11th 1975
McNair, Sue in *Dartford Chronicle* July 7th 1975

19. Richard Nash
Green, Ivan in *Kent Life* June 1991

20. Viscount Northcliffe
Evans, Mary in *Kent Life* April 1978
Broadstairs Society Exhibition information sheet July 1995
Lapthorne, W H in *Bygone Kent* Vol 9, No 9

21. Samuel Palmer
Thomas, Denis in *In Britain* October 1977
Edwards, Gwen in *Kent Life* May 1979
Bisson, Joan in *County Magazine* November 1985

22. Major Percy Powell-Cotton
Quex Museum House and Gardens booklet
Evans, Marian in *Kent Life* September 1979

23. Rev James Ramsay

Bradley, Ian in *Kent Life* August 1969
24. Salomons family
Parkes, James *Three David Salomons at Broomhill* booklet
McCooey, Chris *Images of Southborough and High Brooms* Tempus 1998
25. Marcus Samuel
Evans, Marian in *Kent Life* November 1979
Bygone Kent Vol 6, No 2
Obituary *The Times* November 11th 1948
26. Queen Sexburga
Slade, Brian in *Bygone Kent* Vol 13, No 3
Pratt Boorman, H R in *Kent Life* May 1967
Judge, Sheila *The Isle of Sheppey*
27. Saint Simeon
Ritchie, Carson in *Bygone Kent* Vol 12, No 12
Saggi, Rev Louis *Saints of Carmel* Carmelite Institute 1972
28. James Simmons
Panton, Frank *Canterbury's Great Tycoon* Canterbury Society 1990
Hattee, Gerald in *Kentish Gazette* August 24th 1979
Clark, Sydney in *Bygone Kent* Vol 14, No 1
29. Richard Trevithick
Hamilton Jenkin, A K in *The Cornish Review* Summer 1949
Songhurst, Robert in *Kent Life* April 1971
Hodge, James in *Trevithick Society Journal* Vol 1 1973
30. Sir Harry Vane
Winnifrith, Rev A *Men of Kent and Kentish Men* F J Parson 1913
Willcock, John *Life of Sir Harry Vane the Younger* St Catherine's Press 1913
Bradley, Ian in *Kent Life* November 1970
31. Thomas Waghorn
Morrow, Jane in *Kent Life* January 1969
Tomlinson, Norman in *Kent Life* April 1976
32. Dr Dorrit Waterfield
Clements, John in *Kent Life* November 1982
33. H G Wells
Hardwick, Michael and Mollie in *Kent Life* August 1966
MacDougall, Philip in *Bygone Kent* Vol 4, No 1
Davis, Pat in *Kent Life* April 1985
34. Frank Woolley
Preston, Norman *Wisden Cricketers' Almanack* 1979
Bearshaw, Brian *The Big Hitters* Macdonald Queen Anne Press 1986
Tomlinson, Norman in *Kent Life* August 1979

Also used *Dictionary of National Biography;* Simson, Jas *Eminent Men of Kent* 1893.

INDEX

ABOUT THE AUTHOR

Chris McCooey was born and grew up in Kent before spending ten years living and working in Japan and one year studying in California. Returning to England in 1986 with his Japanese wife, Kumiko, and their two children, he lives in a 16th century cottage just outside Tunbridge Wells. He contributes regularly to the weekend sections of *The Times* and *Financial Times* on food, travel and country matters, as well as writing and publishing local books on Kent and Sussex under his in-print JAK Books. These include *Kent Women, Sussex Women, Kent Heroes, Sussex Heroes, Kent Characters* and *Sussex Characters.*